The Syria Dispatches

by

Ming Lauren Holden

with "Guest Dispatcher"

Abu Faisal

These writings came out of a journey I took to Turkey and Syria in 2013. That journey, and this publication, was made possible by the donors to my 2013 Kickstarter campaign entitled "The Search for Syrian Refugees and their Stories". All those who pitched in at least $25 are receiving at least one of these publications as part of their reward. I am entirely indebted to your support and generosity.

Portions of these writings form the shorter essay "The Surest Way To Survive", which won the Honorable Mention in *Crab Orchard Review*'s annual nonfiction contest. That essay is available in the *Review*'s Spring 2015 issue. My continued and profuse thanks to my donors, who waited longer to receive *this* publication as a result of the wait-for-reversion-of-publication-rights associated with *that* publication.

for Ghazi

The Syria Dispatches

Dispatch # 1
~ Sent July 17th, 2013

First, there's the warm air. Then the strong sunlight. Then the quiet balcony, shading a long white plastic table. Then the shapes and colors of the food: bright red cuts of tomato, cucumber, hummus, dark shiny olives. Then the garden outside, a modest plot with hopeful green stalks.

A block away, next to a paved road, rises a hill. The hill is a summer sort of light-brown.

There's shuffling and murmuring. Bread coming in wide discs and torn off by hand. Then the hands doing the tearing, some young, some scarred, some old. A handsome young man sits to your right, with a smile like your old childhood friend Gabe. He laughs at you trying to fit too much into your mouth at once. A quiet man with white hair leans back, looking at his hands grasped in his lap. Four more guys in their late twenties dig in, pouring Coke for everybody and passing plates, conversing quietly in Arabic.

The silence presses in, as though the sunlight itself enforced it. When it isn't very windy, it's very still. A cat noses the crumbling sidewalk below, near a pile of plaster limbs.

Only now feed yourself another bit of the story. The man your age who looks and grins like Gabe, who asks for a picture with you, adjusts his torso in his wheelchair. He shakes the stump coming from his hip as though he usually tapped his foot, as though it were a habit of his, before his legs were blown off by one of Assad's shells. His hands are that graceful because he was a barber, standing in front of his shop when the shell hit eight months ago. The quiet, white haired man -- give him eight years in a cell in the 80s. Add that history to him, unseen and unverified.

And make the hill a few hundred feet off, the one that looks like it could be California wine country: draw a border, an invisible border, halfway up the hill, and call the country beyond Syria.

I am in Reyhanli, a tiny town in Turkey right on the Syrian border that only became known when three bombs went off here in a coordinated attack in May. Abu Faisal, the man who offered to take me into Syria, asks me to lock the metal bar above our knees into place, securing us in our seats as best as we can be secured. Across from us his cousin, Abu Abdo Al Halabi, who is recognizable by his serious unibrow, does the same in the seat he shares a surgeon who fled Damascus after being forced to treat six of Assad's soldiers at gunpoint. Behind them are two more extended family members, a fifteen-year-old girl called Fatima and a 20-year-old young man called Omar who was recently released from one of Assad's jails. Omar had to pretend little connection with his own brother, Mohamed, in order to get out of that jail: after eight months Mohamed is still in what's called "The Palestinian Security Branch", the one of Assad's jails most famous for being a torture center. (Omar has a picture of Mohamed on his PC laptop as the desktop background, along with the date of Mohamed's capture.)

The engine clanks to life and my heart begins racing. It thumps harder when the huge contraption of metal and tires under us begins to move through the evening breeze.

"I've never done this before," I breathe to Abu Faisal, though I suspect that's obvious. I grip the bar and look around, wondering what to focus on so I don't get more sick as we pick up speed.

Fatima produces her iphone, trains it on me, and grins at my expression. The surgeon, who is handsome enough to be on the cast of *Grey's Anatomy*, smiles at me too. "Looks like I chose the wrong night to wear a skirt," I say to Abu Faisal, who chuckles.

I tuck my skirt on either side of my thighs as best I can, then let out an involuntary whoop as the boat ride picks up speed, rocking us up and down through the air, above the game booths and the children's car carousel and the pepper trees shuddering in the wind.

*

Dr. Mahrouz spent around six months with Bashar Assad a few decades back when they were both in medical programs, smoking and playing cards.

"Med school?" I ask when Mahrouz tells me this. "Assad's a doctor?"

"An ophthalmologist!" he says. "How did you not know Assad is an ophthalmologist? You know nothing."

"I don't know anything," I agree. "I'm not a journalist. I haven't researched much."

The quiet older man to my left, who was part of the Muslim Brotherhood before becoming disillusioned with it in the 80s and spending nearly a decade in jail, says something to Mahrouz, who translates: "He is saying you should cover up in the camp."

"I brought scarves and long sleeves," I say. "I didn't think I needed to wear them today. Would you prefer I put them on?"

"No, no, we don't mind," says Mahrouz. "In fact we are thoroughly enjoying it."

Mahrouz, a Syrian cardiologist based in the U.K., has never met a vegetable he doesn't like. He keeps dashing off when we're walking to or from dinner in Reyhanli to buy or uproot one (or three). He tells me that our motley crew's Muslim guys are lucky I don't understand Arabic. He explains the Muslim afterlife thusly: "A river of wine! So many women, and the ugliest one is more beautiful than Angelina Jolie!"

Mahrouz goes into Syria once every one or two months to deliver aid. His mother still lives in his village of Maaret Al Nouman. He and his brother Ahmed, who is the commander of Maaret's Free Syrian Army unit, are carrying the village on their shoulders. Today in the upstairs portion of a prosthetic limb center in Reyhanli, where the families of amputees stay while their loved ones are fitted and rehabilitated and where we are all sleeping, Mahrouz hands me a passport-size photo of himself in uniform. In it his hair is darker, but he has remained handsome even in his middle age. The problem is, he knows it. This is why, when he hears I am undecided about crossing the border into Syria, he sits next to me and lowers his voice to a suggestive level.

"You know," he purrs, "once you go into the camp you might realize that you like it and are not as afraid as you might think. The feeling when you go further into Syria, with everything happening, can be...well, it can be exciting."

He raises an eyebrow, smirking.

Abu Faisal was just warning me about this twenty minutes ago, when he came into the room we girls sleep in for his shower stuff from the balcony, where he spent the night with Abu Abdo Al Halabi (his impressively-unibrowed cousin). "Honestly, *I* wouldn't go further into Syria if I were you," he said, shaking his head in his basketball shorts and shower sandals, holding a ziplock bag of deodorant and shampoo. "The guys out there in the living room, they'll try to convince you to go. But it actually is dangerous—more so than two months ago, which is the last time I went."

Next to me on the sofa, Mahrouz, amazingly enough, isn't talking. For perhaps the first and only time, he's actually waiting for my response.

I'm a creative writer and not a journalist, a post-conflict development worker with no conflict zone experience and none of the street smarts required for it. I'm not army or CIA material. I have no poker face and all the diplomatic discretion of Honey-Boo-Boo. Blonde-haired, blue-eyed, the baby of the family, a perennial leaver-of-towels-on-other-people's-beds, I jump at the slightest noise. Even to cross the border about twenty meters into Atmeh "Olive Tree" refugee camp is a technically illegal move, and as America cut diplomatic ties with Syria, my government could do nothing for me if I were captured. Even to cross the border at all is, technically, to enter a war zone.

"I'll think about it," I tell Mahrouz.

Dispatch # 2
~ Sent July 21st, 2013

We've all got long, lightweight pants and closed-toed shoes. I have a scarf to tie over my head later, since I'm the only girl light and blonde enough to stand out. There are passports, cameras that can be stowed away in our backs and backpacks, and big bottles of water from the shop across the way where Adriana has just disappeared for some almonds to pass around as we wait. It's a bright, warm morning that promises a brutally hot day.

We're a motley crew, together to cross the border. There's Mahrouz, the cardiologist from Syria who is based in the U.K. There's his fifteen-year-old daughter Fatima, who is going to get "work experience" credit from her school for this. There's Abu Faisal, the thirty-one-year old Syrian dude based in Abu Dhabi who sounds like he's from my area of Southern California and who is, through an invitation he extended to me after reading about my Kickstarter, responsible for my presence in the group. There's his twenty-seven-year-old cousin Abu Abdo Al Halabi, who is not telling his dad--who's still in Aleppo-- that he's been risking his life to come into Syria to deliver aid because then, of course, his dad would kill him (this he says grinning). There's Dr Khawla, who does a rotation of four weeks in Syria and one week at home in Ohio with her three kids; she does this using her own money, without resources from the official association of Syrian medics of which she's a board member. She will tell the Free Syrian Army checkpoint people that we're crossing with her to deliver medical aid. And there's Adriana, a young American documentarian with a masters in global development and peace studies who recently moved to Beirut. We're waiting for our vehicles.

There are two more blondes, actually, who jumped on board in the eleventh hour. At the cheapest-I-could-find hostel in Istanbul, where I recovered from jet lag before traveling here to Reyhanli, I met a couple of personable cousins from

Scotland and France. Vincent was a photographer, and John was, as it turned out there in our random one-out-of-hundreds-of-hostels-in-Taksim, journalist John Beck, who'd written on regional topics for *Business Insider* and the *Daily Beast*. I emailed Abu Faisal right there from the hostel kitchen, knowing he wanted as much light thrown on the situation as possible, asking if he'd like to be put in contact with John. "The more the merrier!" Abu Faisal responded. And so, yesterday I waited with the Abus and Marhouz and the girls in the slanting evening light at a central intersection of tiny Reyhanli for these two skinny blonde guys in matching button-up denim shirts and black skinny jeans to hop off a bus from Antakya. They really did look like they were hopping off a tour bus, like indie-boy-band-goes-to-Syria.

This morning, as we wait for the vehicles to fit all of us for the trip across the border, John the journalist's French cousin Vincent the photographer is standing in the shade of a stone wall in his trendy Ray-Bans, describing the editor of a European magazine: "He didn't want photos of starving children only. He wanted photos of starving children with parasites that would swell the bellies. You know what he actually said? 'Their bellies aren't swollen. These kids don't look starving enough. They don't look enough like they're dying.'"

*

War is, 99% of the time, a very quiet life, I will realize. Waiting is the primary activity of people in a war zone when those people happen not to be in the places getting the shit shelled out of them. When the world isn't suddenly and irrevocably swallowed in a melee of explosive fire, and children's intestines aren't strewn on the concrete outside neighborhood shops, the days simply stretch on like deserts, long and incredibly silent. "There's no *light*," Abu Faisal said emphatically on my first day in Reyhanli. "Usually for people working inside--people living inside--people still inside--they don't have jobs, they're kids aren't in school or anything:

sometimes what keeps them going is they 'll see a little light at the end of the tunnel and be like, 'Oh, its gonna get better because so and so is helping us, this is gonna happen.' But there's no light, and they're still working, they're still like, 'No, we believe in the revolution, we believe in whats happening,' but their kids are being lost and theres no light, meaning there's just this huge depression, this huge hopelessness, asking, 'When will it end?'"

*

My friend David wrote to me recently: "All afternoon, juxtapositions of other places I have been, other people I've known, wafted through memory like wisps of smoke."

I don't think I can put it better. For some reason, other experiences I have had working abroad—Ecuador, Bolivia, China, Mongolia, Russia, Kenya—have appeared during this stint, rushing up or just hanging in the warm Mediterranean breeze right outside my field of vision. I feel a strong sense of duty to report back, as I said I would. I continue to believe in the sacred nature of bearing witness to the lives and suffering of others. But there are other natures. It is the murkier aspect of witness which is at issue, as I turn to my keyboard and attempt to type home to you about Syria. The concept and practice of bearing witness is part and parcel of the web of privilege ensnaring any attempt to bear that witness (I "bear" little, comparatively speaking), let alone to "report back." I've come to the conclusion that to write responsibly about this conflict (as well as, perhaps, any conflict, development and suffering in general) I must not edit out those associative memories. I must take responsibility for the filters and blinders which my experiences have both removed and given. Because the people in these pages are real ones, because the conflict in which some are fatally trapped so fraught and bloody, I'll have to be a character in this story, because in so doing, I admit that the eyeball isn't omniscient and Emersonian. It's mine, with the imperfections, aberrations, and associations that come with a fallible medium. In the

7

name of the people who are dying needlessly, I will not pretend otherwise. I am not an omniscient narrator, and my body is a product of privilege and its attendant luck and it's a thing, here, in this narrative: it's how I got there, how I was physically present, and I see no ethical way to write it out.

Because this journey was prompted both by what I saw in the mainstream media of Syria (harrowing conditions for refugees) and what I didn't see (much else about those refugees--or much about anything, really, besides lurid videos of extremist violence), I will also occasionally reference other pieces about Syria in these ones. For instance, a departure from that carnage-centric media norm is the recent account from wildly brave journalist Francesca Borri: devastating both because of what she writes from a bunker in Aleppo- "Syria isn't Syria anymore. It is a nuthouse"--and because of the editor who told her that he wasn't interested in a six thousand word piece from the front lines if no one dies anywhere in those words.

*

Charged with introducing right-eyed eighteen-year-olds in a sleepy Indiana town two years ago to composition, I chose to assign them from the requisite book "Eating The Other: Desire and Resistance" by bell hooks. An incredibly dense essay with such a high register of diction was no one's favorite, of course, but it was a meaty addition to the readings from which my students crafted their final analysis papers. I remember pondering with them: what does this consumption metaphor mean? If what bell hooks references is not straight-up cannibalism, how does consuming what is different take place? What is hooks saying that she couldn't say without such a lens? That photography editor Vincent describes and the one Borri dealt with: they make no apologies for equating readers and viewers of media with *consumers*. My own culture spent the first decade since the turn of the century, the years overshadowed by Iraq and Afghanistan, weirdly obsessed with vampires, as evidenced by the hit show *True*

Blood. Now it's obsessed with medieval battles for the seven kingdoms in *Game of Thrones*, a show whose pilot episode featured gladiator-eqsue wedding rituals replete with the same spilling-out of intestines visible in videos of Syrian childrens' deaths. Both of these "shows" "premiered" at about the same time, too. I wasn't processing the manslaughter in Syria. I could digest the manslaughter when it was fake, and enjoy consuming such scenes without faulting myself morally for that enjoyment. And thus began what I think any self-consciousness with respect to "someone else's" war engenders: a long process of familiarizing myself with surrogacy. With what it means, how we enact it, how we let others do it for us, and the limits of human compassion—the limits of our digestion of the suffering of others, of their humanity-- surrogacy illuminates. The phrase "proxy war," in other words, could be a more inclusive term than it is, if we as spectators are going to be honest about our role—or lack thereof—in all of this.

This is why I pause before relating the tiny slice of Syrians' suffering I saw, why these first two dispatches aren't chock-full of horrific stories and garish imagery. To what end would I tell you that story? No one has decided or not decided to do or not do anything about Syria for lack of horrific visuals, torrid tales, and devastating statistics. I could tell you about the suffering, but we've all already *seen* it on our screens. We all ate that already.

Of course, I will tell you what I saw. I simply realized, when I thought about how to ethically engage with the relation of trauma that is neither mine nor yours, that I needed to take a breath and consider the lens with which to do so.

*

Evening on the balcony after the day trip into Syria, and we're all tuckered out. Abu Abdo Al Halabi is showing me a video of monkeys on the hood of a car. He doesn't prepare me for what's coming, and is looking sideways at me to watch my polite smile morph into a "o" of surprise and then emit a loud cackle. Someone took the video with their phone when a monkey ran out of the roadside greenery and jumped onto the hood of their car—laughing is audible in the background—and kept filming when yet another monkey hopped aboard the car hood and proceeded to hump the living shit out of the first monkey, to the screaming delight of the video's car passengers —and, now, to me. Even Adriana, the documentarian from Connecticut, who is much more reserved and graceful than I am (her preternatural calm amid a hurried exit from Maarat due to heavy shelling the last time she accompanied the men into Syria earned her the nickname "CIA"), is snickering into her hand as she looks over Abu Abdo Al Halabi's shoulder. Fatima, Mahrouz's teenaged daughter, is sitting next to her father and looks over at us with interest. "Whot're you watching? Can I see?" she asks in her London accent. Adriana and I widen our eyes.

"That's up to your dad, I think," I say, sympathizing with how annoying this must be for her to hear. Fatima, whose hair is long and thick and up in a ponytail and who sprinkles what she says with "D'y'know whot I mean?" has a father who travels into Syria amid certain shelling monthly, sure, but she's comfortingly, very, fifteen, a mix of childlike goofiness and awkward comments coupled with the kind of killer smile and fledgeling beauty that occasions her soliciting advice on how see-through her top is before joining her male family members on the balcony. "I'd never hear the end of it from my cousins out there," she'd said, gesturing with her thumb to the balcony as we changed out of the clothes we'd worn across the border. Now that we'd receded from the company of young FSA men in pink sorority T shirts holding large guns and the crackling tensity of the air at the border checkpoint, her concerns were once again pedestrian.

Truth be told, the concerns are pedestrian within the camp. The concerns are pedestrian everywhere in Syria, because civilians have realized, as they did in 1940s Europe, that the show must go on. People got together and danced in basements during WWII amid the threat and event of bombing because life had, still, to be lived.

Dispatch # 3
~ Sent July 29th, 2013

Maya Angelou said once, about adulthood: "Most people don't grow up. It's too damn difficult. What happens is most people get older. That's the truth of it. They honor their credit cards, they find parking spaces, they marry, they have the nerve to have children, but they don't grow up. Not really. They get older. But to grow up costs the earth, the earth. It means you take responsibility for the time you take up, for the space you occupy. It's serious business. And you find out what it costs us to love and to lose, to dare and to fail. And maybe even more, to succeed. What it costs, in truth. Not superficial costs—anybody can have that—I mean in truth. That's what I write. What it really is like. I'm just telling a very simple story."

In the office/spare room of my cousin Cliff's house in Oakland, California, the woman with the eyes is there, watching me as I sleep, watching me like a hawk. She watches over the wonderful guest bed, the bed that has a memory foam mattress and is covered in Siamese kitty hair (and sometimes the kitties themselves, if I am lucky). I have woken up by the woman with the eyes in Cliff's house at least once a year for a decade now; I first visited him and his partner Dorothy when I was eighteen, after my first semester of college. These visits to them became a mainstay. I watched their lives arc through engagement to marriage to child number one and child number two; I helped them move from a little house in the Castro to a slightly larger one in Oakland; I watched Cliff's garden grow a little bigger every year, the wee greenhouse pungent with tomato plants. They let me observe them be grown-ups; they explained patiently the aspects of this whole adulthood business that stumped me so. Their children, Penelope and Brian, are the first ones I've known well since they were born as I myself am the last cousin in my generation to come along. Penelope, who is six, is a big-emotion-haver and also brilliant at everything from backflips to thousand-piece lego sets; her little brother Brian, who's four, is a mellow dude with a wicked sense of humor and a perfect accent when he pronounces Spanish words. Their parents met in college and feed them food from Trader Joe's and work excessively at their jobs as engineer and consultant to give their children what all children deserve. The little I understand about family and adulthood and emotionally responsible parenting I learned from Cliff and Dorothy.

You've probably seen the woman with the eyes, who has been made an example of. Her eyes are green. There's a rust-colored headscarf lightly wrapped around her head but not covering so much that we can't see her brown hair. The photo of the woman with the eyes, known generally as "The Afghan Girl," has always been in the guest room, since 2002 when I started visiting Cliff and Dorothy. It's framed and I remember Dorothy once called her "stunning," which about summed it up. (Even Mindy Kaling, an American comedy actress, mentions her in recent a *New Yorker* piece as "the *National Geographic* girl with the crazy penetrating eyes.") If one day I returned and the photo had gone, I would miss it. I can't remember if I saw the photo before that, but I saw it years after, in a lesson plan in graduate school. We were to show it to our elementary composition students for their photo analysis lesson. The woman with the eyes was the example of "demand." There is offer, and there is demand. If the subject is staring at the camera, the subject is demanding something.

The portrait of the woman with the eyes was taken in Pakistan in 1984 by Steve McCurry. There was "a haunted look" in her eyes, McCurry would say later, so he got her permission to photograph her. She was twelve or so. She'd made the two-week trek to Nasir Bagh refugee camp on the Afghanistan-Pakistan border after the Soviet invasion that killed her parents. She had come with her siblings around the age of six here on a trek that was often itself a fatal journey. It was snowy and they would hide in caves if jets came and beg for blankets. That haunted look seemed representative of her struggle and that of the refugees McCurry saw in the camp. His photograph of her became the most recognizable one in the history of the *National Geographic* and letters poured in in a steady stream over the next seventeen years. Some people committed to work in Pakistan in refugee camps because of that photo. People wanted to adopt her. Sponsor her. Marry her.

The photo was used on promotional Amnesty International materials during those seventeen years. Her photo is so iconic as to feature on the cover of the commemorative "Special Members Edition" of *National Geographic*. The young woman herself had no idea, for almost twenty years, that she was famous. She didn't see the picture until 2002. Perhaps she is not a Special Member.

By 2002, when she saw the only photo ever taken of herself, she had borne four daughters, not all of whom survived. She had been called the Mona Lisa of the Twentieth Century.

But her name isn't Mona Lisa. It's Sharbat.

*

This is all to say that in the Atmeh "Olive Tree" Camp, in Syria, there was a girl.

*

In her poem "Trillium," Louise Gluck wrote: "I knew nothing; I could do nothing but see." As we crossed the border into Syria, I remembered those lines, which seem to me like birth, like what babies experience. If I had known nothing of the violence erupting unpredictably that had brought these people here, to a baking-hot day in July, the children hoping for photos and candy, the men with arresting sea-green eyes and dirt-tinted skin: would I have sensed war and tension? How much was I imposing a story onto a group of people standing in the sun—the story I'd been told and fed in tiny bits that didn't always add up, bits I'd been fed by news sites, by articles, by Americans, by Turks, by Syrians, by twitter feeds? I felt nervous, thought "war zone," made an association that was not based on my experience at all, not on my seen evidence. There *was* no seen evidence.

Atmeh "Olive Tree" camp is about fifty meters over the Turkish border into Syria. In it live some of the poorest Syrians, but the luckiest of the poorest: the ones who could get out of Damascus, Aleppo, Homs. And yet they are the unluckiest of the lucky: they can't afford paper documentation, so they can't legally get over the border because by the end of 2011 Turkey had closed its borders to paperless refugees. Atmeh camp has yet to be shelled, but Assad's jets did fly overhead here late last year. "Olive tree" because there are olive trees in every direction—and for me they are what make this land different from the land I came from, wine country in southern California, because the olive trees are different than the oaks when nothing else is different about the land, not the color of the grass or its dry-oatweed smell. The olive trees are such a bleached, dusty green, like original Wrigley's chewing gum, that the whole scene is whitewashed—the pale clouds and pale sky and pale trees and pale grayish makeshift tents of a city of 25,000 people who weren't here a year or two ago.

As Atmeh camp is on the Syrian side of the border, its UNHCR-emblem-stamped tents are kind of contraband. The UNHCR can't enter Syria except at the request of Assad. That's kind of a complication; Assad, of course, doesn't want to shelter these people, he wants to kill them. When Angelina Jolie visited Syrian refugees as an official UNHCR envoy, she visited them in Jordan. So did John Kerry a week or two ago. The tents that Maram Foundation founder Yakzan, who tours the camp with us, secured for the camp he had to secure by creating the Maram Foundation in the first place, then receiving the tents in Turkey via a network of other aid agencies, ultimately bringing them over the border himself.

The tents, the ones with blue UNHCR-stamped emblems, are what constitute the classrooms of the makeshift camp school, like the makeshift camp school in which McCurry found twelve-year-old Sharbat with the haunted look in her eyes that came to symbolize the plight of the refugee. He didn't describe her as "demanding." She was, in fact, shy, and so he approached her last, there in the school tent.

This is what the *National Geographic* says of the article that accompanied Sharbat's famous photo: "A stalemated war that has killed countless civilians and forced a quarter of the population into exile." It could well be what accompanies this writing, about Syria in 2013. Syria has morphed into a situation that looks to be even worse, in terms of length and casualties and displacement, than the one in Afghanistan at the end of the last century. Elliot Higgins, a self-trained Syrian weapons tracker who analyzes footage on youtube of the war's various groups, put it simply in an interview with me earlier this summer: "They're going to be refugees for a very long time."

The universal blue UNHCR emblem stamping the contraband tents looks like this: a person shielded by two hands. And around this, the person and hands, a ring of olive tree branches.

*

What I mean to say is that the girl, who was the most beautiful girl, she carried a candy bar next to me in the heat for two hours as we toured the camp. I stole glances at her often, beside me. Thick brows, brown skin, brown hair, deep brown eyes, pointed chin. Her face might be the most gorgeous face I've seen on someone her age—she's probably not older than six or seven, around Penelope's age. But she's not cute, she's gorgeous. Like the models on Fashion TV. She wanted me to buy the candy bar. I didn't. I could have. More children would have come, perhaps started to fight. It happened when Dr. Mahrouz gave them chocolate.

We spoke with some of the young people at the school. Their faces were expressive, mischievous, shy. They wanted to practice English. They wanted to know why we weren't Muslim. The littlest children sang for us. Deeper into the country, on bombed-out streets, the lost generation of Syrians, their peers, roam the streets in their third year without proper schooling. More and more of them are joining various military factions (read: any regular Syrian dudes with any guns) that dissolve and attribute loyalty to whoever can pay them a salary and decisively arm them, who—unless and until Obama and his friends take action--are chiefly wealthy private donors from the gulf countries (read: very religious). More and more of Syria's youth are set to grow up angry, illiterate, and traumatized. No school, no routine, family dead, danger, bombs, nightmares daily, broken promises: phenomenally damaged nervous systems affecting for the worse the lifelong ability to settle down, to sleep, to digest, to think things through, to be functional citizens in any way.

This bleak future is settling in as though it is an inevitability. It is not, but to admit that I must admit how I take painkillers for my headache after the day in the sun, after seeing her and enjoying her gorgeous face as I refused her a coin, after I take a long hot shower and wash the dust of a place with no sewage system off of my shoes. We all know there are beautiful children refugees who are being killed, both slowly and quickly. Words like "suffering," we say in writing workshop, stand in for something else. Go for an arresting image, we advise each other, like the picture of the refugee woman on *National Geographic,* who is not offering, she's demanding. She went on to have "a very hard life." That's a stand-in for something too. *National Geographic* began an Afghan Children's Fund in her name, which is a small bright nugget I alight onto like a thirsty butterfly as though because of it I'm called upon to do less. I will not forget the girl I gave no money to. I did not ask her name. I did not take her picture. Her life is too likely not to benefit from how compelling her marble-dark eyes and pointed chin and brown hair are. If I take her photo and show it to you, we will witness her beauty, and it's not that we'll be without compassion. It's that Sharbat's skin turned leathery, her daughter died, she had to walk three dangerous hours and drive another six from her remote Afghan village at the turn of the century to be reunited with the lauded photographer who took the heretofore only existent photograph of her, the one millions of people had seen that she herself hadn't.

It's that whatever Sharbat's green eyes demanded, in the photo we all consumed: we didn't give it to her.

*

I realize, slowly, what it will take. And I am afraid to tell you. I am afraid to ask this of myself.

I realize it when my plane touches down in Hatay, Turkey to meet Abu Faisal and travel with him to the border; the air is so fresh, so humid there in the morning and the pale sweptness of the landscape reminds me of a trip I took in 2008. A trip on the last leg of the Trans-Siberian railway to Inner Mongolia, China, where there lived the wife of an exiled writer I was advocating for back in Ulaanbaatar, (Outer) Mongolia. He'd been driven out. His wife and daughter remained there in China, in Inner Mongolia. They had strip-searched her at the border when she visited him, they had ransacked his office. He sent me onto the dusty train with toothpaste and wine for her. He had arranged for his doctor friend to have lunch with me on the first long stop inside China. The whole sky was white with Gobi silt at the stop and the doctor's daughter tapped around in red shoes with a dog that looked like a white mop.

As with anyone coping with a loss, on some days in Ulaanabaatar the exiled writer was optimistic that he'd get out, that he'd get them out, his wife and daughter. Some days he was inconsolable. I can't eat alone, he'd say. His wife would echo exactly he same thing when I stayed with her. It's not right, they both said, it's not natural, to have a family and then not have one.

There was one refrain in my mind, as I showered the dust off in his wife's home in Hohhot, his old home, as she prepared mutton leg: *This is where he cannot be. This is where he cannot be.*

I realize it when I ride in the early morning with Abu Faisal away from the airport in Turkey toward the Syrian border, and I am reminded by the nature of the sunlight and the geological landscape of Santa Maria, the closest city to my childhood home in California. And then, when I am walking with the larger-than-life Dr. Mahrouz the Syrian cardiologist who now lives in the U.K. and comes back monthly to deliver aid, on our first night all gathered in Reyhanli, in a high breeze on the main road in and out of town--it's after dinner, the breeze smells familiar, even the road is familiar, and we're headed back to the prosthetic limb center where we sleep and where there is being rehabilitated a handsome young Syrian man who looks like my childhood friend Gabe and who lost his legs to Assad's shells—Mahrouz is telling me by the roadside, after trotting to catch up with us because he stopped to investigate an opportunity to buy tomatoes and cucumber at a little stand, he's telling me of his time at school with Assad and the nature of Assad's megalomania: that Assad will raze his own people, crazed, until none of them exist before he surrenders because they are all his, the country is his, he is entitled to it and he won't stop—and I think of Highway 101, how this road is the Highway 101 of this place.

And I will have to *make* it the 101. I will have to make it my family. My home. I will have to tell you—by which I mean tell myself, to understand it--that way. I am going to have to pick my favorite children in the world—Penelope and Brian, who before I left San Francisco (I left out of there and not LAX in part so I could see them, before and after) piled on top of me in the hammock in the sun by their dad's garden in Oakland, who brought me raspberries cupped in their fingers, Penny with her impish eye gleam and Brian with his face-creases in the morning, who draw with sidewalk chalk in

19

matching tie-dye outfits and lay hands on my forearms as I read them stories—and you're going to have to pick yours.

And they're going to have to die.

Dispatch # 4
~Sent August 7th, 2013

The vineyards that surround my parents' ranch in Santa Barbara County, California, have been abandoned, and only drying grapevines remain. Rebels have taken up neighboring abandoned mansions as bases and used the wine cellars as stockpiling rooms and barracks. Most irrigation has long since been switched off, since Obama's strongholds span the agricultural basin in central inland California where there used to grow a huge percentage of America's produce and where the California state water project is based. The shortage is felt throughout rebel-held territory, where canned goods were stored by sensible people who were branded as pessimists when the protests began. Those pessimists are now making a handy profit, though as the value of the US dollar descends into freefall, they demand payment of other in-kind goods more and more often.

I drove upstate in one of my parents' old ranch vehicles, a dirty jeep covered in hay bits and smelling of mice in the AC vents, to bring Penelope and Brian down here on one of the last days the 101 was even vaguely passable, right before the opposition lost the Bay Area to the government army. Their parents, my cousin Cliff and his wife Dorothy, who let me watch them be adults and ask big life-questions as they hosted me every year over the last decade, were blown apart by a shell as Cliff dropped Dorothy off at the train station so she could attend a hearing in Sacramento as an environmental consultant. It was one of the first shells to fall in a days-long attack. We were caught unawares; we thought Obama's forces were going to attack Los Angeles first, and in any place that isn't under attack, people attempt to conduct business as usual —as usual as possible. So they dropped off the kids, and drove to the train station, where Cliff died instantly in the explosion and Dorothy bled out slowly, trapped under a fallen pillar. She knew, in her last moments, why no one helped her: by then we'd all heard that a second shell follows the first, to kill those who would run to the first victims.

It took some bribing and a few stretches of driving off-road both ways—Highway 101 was impassable in some places, littered with decaying body parts and exploded concrete and "checkpoints" of escaped prison convicts who claimed to be part of the rebel army—but I managed to get Penelope and Brian back to the ranch, which had become our family's base of operations since my parents' siblings and all their children were in urban areas when the protests began. I found Penelope and Brian late the night of their parents' death, finally asleep at their kind neighbor's house in Oakland. The rebels almost didn't let me into Oakland until I showed them pictures of the kids and begged while across the water, in the heart of San Francisco, flames lit up the nigh sky. As their neighbor helped me load the car with Cliff and Dorothy's important documents, the contents of their dry pantry, and the kids' belongings, we could feel the explosions reverberate, shaking the flower vase on the windowsill. The kids, exhausted from wailing, were somehow sound asleep, and I hoped that when they woke up, they would be on the ranch, and my mother would be there to talk them into the first steps they had to make forward into a strange life without their parents in this place where the plants were dying.

*

The protests began peacefully enough – the Occupy demonstrations, and the flagrant use of tear gas by police officers at those demonstrations a couple years back, prepared us for the reality that there would be protests in response to the Snowden leaks and that there would be local law enforcement crackdowns in response. But nothing prepared us for the news of the sheer extent of the NSA surveillance or the outpouring of demonstrators who took to the streets to voice their dissent. Twitter and Facebook enabled a coordinated protest in every major city in America with only a few hours of notice. It was an odd union of bedfellows; the Libertarians with their rifles wanting the government out of their house alongside Democrats who were appalled at the abuse of executive power. The streets were packed with people from all political, ethnic, and religious backgrounds and the electricity in the air from the sheer force of collective human will was palpable. Such unifying power the people of America, this generation of Americans, hadn't felt before and it was contagious, empowering, thrilling. A total of 100 million people were reported to pack the streets of every urban space in America, hollering for their nation to change hands, for the government to restore democracy.

Too many discrete incidents occurred for anyone to know how it began, which match was first struck, for anyone to be able to explain what happened as though one story could isolate it – as though one narrative could effectively encapsulate the implosion of a nation.

First came news of gang rapes. In New Orleans, in Dallas, in the Bronx, in Los Angeles. Then there were bank robberies. There were black blocs of kids in San Francisco and Chicago with matching scarves wrapped around their mouths, readying themselves for tear gas and packing their backpacks with rocks they'd send into the windows of government offices, of Saks Fifth Avenue, and of large, pretty houses. There were lethal shoot-outs at fifty meters' distance between cops and civilians in St Louis, in Kansas City, in Las Vegas, in Orlando, in Minneapolis. Often gangs became the de facto lawmakers; in certain areas, they had been all along. Places like Compton and Richmond, for this reason, held out the longest against the government, though its denizens were no less fearful than they'd been before. Gallows humor prevailed in the poorest areas, on reservations and in housing projects nationwide, as residents told one another with sad smiles that they had been trained for what looked to be a decades-long war. A war that would tear at the social, economic, familial, religious, and political fabric of what was once a great nation, decimating every facet of its infrastructure in such a way that it would be generations before recovery could truly begin.

Though the vineyards were dying out by the time they
got here, Penelope and Brian, my six- and four- year old
cousins from Oakland, proved themselves awfully good at
foraging the remaining grapes, because they grew up picking
berries in their dad's garden. We tried for at least one of us to
be watching them at first, but as things got worse we had to
leave it to Penelope to grow up enough to take care of her little
brother without someone older there to kiss her elbow scrapes
or soothe his cries. Civic structure, like police, had long since
disappeared, and so when there weren't angry young men
patrolling our stretch of Foxen Canyon Road in packs,
crowding into the backs of trucks and ransacking nearby
wealthy actors' weekend homes and winemakers' villas,
Penelope and Brian would come out from a lean-to where they
hid and they looked for grapes. They called themselves rebels,
those guys ransacking houses, so to the wider world we were
part of their group--but they were still the kind of guys I
trained Penelope and Brian to hide from, holding their warm
bodies close in the lean-to and putting a finger over my lips.

When they hid, they hid from some of our closest family
friends from our pre-war life. My brother's best friend Len was
big brother to my own best friend, Bea. The boys home-
schooled together for a year when they were eleven and
learned to build stanchions and milk goats in 4H. Our mother,
who is seventy, learned alongside him and after the war began
she kept the goat's grandkids alive, milked them daily,
strained the cheese, scanned the skies for jets. Her son, my
brother, by then a doctor, was somewhere in Oregon, which
was unreachable, and she lived in Los Alamos—the little one in
California, not the big one in New Mexico. That's where the
ranch was, where Penelope and Brian and I were.

In the first days of the war, Bea and I didn't feel it much
—it wasn't our houses, wasn't our families. Then people
started talking about genocide, the week before we were to

shop for Bea's wedding dress. The day of our date, I waited at our old carpool spot beside the 101 in the heat, texting and calling. No answer. Sometime that afternoon, a huge tank rumbled by. I jumped the white fence under the billboard on which a cowboy lassoed the words "Welcome to Los Alamos" and hid in the brush, hoping they wouldn't notice the dusty car in the shade. Thankfully the tank passed. They weren't going for Foxen Canyon--not today. But my stomach started to hurt as I realized that this meant Los Alamos was a no-go, and I understood that Bea, with whom I would chant "the mountains are following us!" on the way to school every day when we were small, could not my friend anymore, and that although she was a mile away in Los Alamos, I'd probably never see her again.

*

The anti-NSA-surveillance demonstrations began, ironically, as a unifying desire for justice to be served in the face of blatant executive violations of democracy, but as bloodshed escalated, feuds and divisions that had been buried (partially, at least) for decades re-emerged, and the most-dreaded nightmare burgeoned: America divided violently along religious and racial lines, with civil war the immediate and seemingly endless result. We lost half our family friends this way, after the shelling wouldn't let up and Obama made it clear that his being Protestant determined it all: that Protestants couldn't be friends with anyone else, that *theirs* was the chosen party to lead the nation, that *they* were the only people Obama would refer to as Americans. Muslims were found murdered in their beds; friendships between Jews and Christians, of course, were also out of the question. Our Catholic winemaker neighbors were taken out for "questioning" by Obama's forces early on in the war, and Bea and Len, who had been raised Protestant, were drafted into military service by the government the day that tank rolled in.

Once a schoolteacher, my mother has a big heart and allowed several once-distant Catholic acquaintances to hide in the gulch that's littered with lupines in the spring, where my father roped a tire swing up for me from an oak branch in the 90s. We pleaded with her not to harbor refugees on the ranch, but she said she'd rather die in dignity than refuse good people a place to sleep. At dusk she would look up heavily from her garden, which was at the highest vantage point on the ranch, toward the string of lights that was Los Alamos, where our post office box was and where we couldn't go anymore. Undergoing torture at the hands of an extremist rebel faction, Bea's father Jack, a kindly vet who used to look after our animals and who band-aided my knees when I fell on a skateboard in his driveway, finally bleated that my father is Jewish. My mother, who was brought up Episcopalian, and my brother and I were all blacklisted. When Obama's forces didn't have more pressing problems and more full-blooded Jews to focus on, we knew they'd set their sights on us. We didn't begrudge Jack; none of us begrudged anyone else those admissions anymore because we all knew the duress under which such information was given. My mother's best friend Lydia, her colleague at the little country school that hadn't opened its doors in two years, also kept goats and had a garden in Los Alamos. Her son was forced into government service and his legs were blown off within a month. She looked after him, wheeled him around the house. She housed and fed some of her and our mother's old students—the ones caught on the government side—just as our mother did the ones caught on our side. We knew Lynn thought of our mother too, when she gardened and fed the former students they used to team-teach, when she handed them carrots and bags of milk before those former students, now teenagers with acne and braces, would strap guns to themselves and go out on missions from which they were unlikely to return.

Our father disappeared early on, for kindness, for sheltering the first defectors from the local police force, who pitched tents in the dry creek bed at the bottom of our property. We could only hope our father was dead for his charity, and not alive in one of Obama's torture chambers. But my father was a Jew, and the likelihood of his being chained to a boiling pipe too strong for us to sleep well at night. If he was indeed alive, they probably kept him at Lompoc. Lompoc Air Force Base was 25 miles away, and it was the only local stronghold of Obama's that rebels hadn't been able to infiltrate. At night, after Penelope and Brian fell asleep, the Catholics hiding in the creekbed would emerge and we'd study the charts and maps by candlelight, sharing rumors and speculating as to why Obama hadn't ordered the use of the heavy-duty weapons, even atomic weapons, we knew to be stockpiled at Lompoc. Probably because there wasn't a way to spin that to the international press. In spite of Obama shutting down the internet and phone towers –Twitter, Youtube, Facebook, and Instagram being the contemporary enemies of any abusive government – news of the suffering in America had leaked, often in thumb drives filled with handheld video recordings and digital images of the carnage that "runners" smuggled at night to the Mexico or Canada border or to owners of global satellite phones. There were infinite charts out there, of rebel strongholds, of family connections, of disease outbreaks, but one of the most-consulted ones was the chart of satellite phone owners and where they were located— and who they affiliated themselves with. Because the rebels weren't one set and clear group of people but an amorphous spectrum of loosely linked groups. Most of them were the men in each town who banded together to stand guard in shifts when Obama's forces began their systematic slaughtering of non-Protestants. The rebels were regular guys who didn't all believe in the same things and who didn't all vote for the same people. A lot of them were teenagers who didn't know how to use guns.

To say that all of these little clutches of combat rookies, these ragtag bands of local vigilantes, were of a piece was more than a little off, but we didn't know how to convince the international media of that. Neither Mexico nor Canada had stepped in to mitigate the chaos; our NATO allies were somehow undecided on whether or when or how to intervene in a president's slaughter of his own people. They seemed to think that refusing to help Obama, technically the entity that was their NATO ally government, was enough of an action. And in the vacuum left by the federal government presence being driven out and by no strong allies stepping in with aid and arms, the power that rushed in to fill the gap was often decidedly extremist. Mexico, unsettled by a years-long drug war, was through that very war well-armed enough off the record to change the game of the conflict in America through private agreements and transactions. The guns came in the way the marijuana and cocaine came in. Certain conservative clutches were in a position to offer arms to the American rebels, but most of the richest and most powerful private donors would only give arms if their recipients swore allegiance to the Catholic church. The rebels who took the arms had to produce proof: they had to wear bandanas with crosses on them, these guys, many of whom were actually secular and atheist, who used to be truck drivers and landscapists. Now they had to proclaim the greatness of God and the Pope as one of their number filmed the rest with a shaky handheld camera, filmed his comrades in the Catholic militia bandanas throwing grenades and firing bullets across highway 246, where government forces gathered their tanks 50 meters away. Half the time they were coked up on the powder that accompanied the guns from Mexico, and the women and children they claimed to protect were scared shitless of them. The rebels became increasingly psychologically troubled and violent, and some came in from other nations, Catholics who had been waiting for a reason to kill Jews and Muslims and who eagerly called themselves "rebels." Civilians caught in the crossfire prayed every day for the help they thought the international community had guaranteed them, but for two years it hasn't come.

Then Uncle Rory, my dad's bother up in Seattle, got sick. He developed an infection. He needed medicine, a certain antibiotic that had grown scarce in rebel-held areas. Lompoc's military base made the entirety of highway 246 a disaster zone, so we couldn't make it to Santa Barbara anymore for supplies, which were coming in fits and starts off repurposed oil rigs into makeshift ports on what was once the pier at the end of State Street. Even people who weren't shot by Obama's forces on 246 were vulnerable to roving bands of prison inmates from the Lompoc Penitentiary, which was one of the first places where able-bodied young men overran a dwindling security force. Some prisoners joined the rebels, some operated as independent assassins, and some did their best to help without fighting: a convicted felon assisted my mother with the well on the ranch and repaired some broken pipes in the house before homesteading in an abandoned shack on a nearby hillside.

I don't satisfy the visual stereotype of a person of Jewish heritage, so I could still scoot by in some situations if people didn't know me or my family personally. It was pretty clear that if I was willing to allow some of these roving bands of men to do with me what they liked, I could get more protection and perhaps the mobility I needed to scare up some supplies. I might need to let one of them marry me, though it would all be in deed and not word since the courthouses had long since been burned down and marriage licenses were nonexistent. If I did marry a rebel, his brigade would allow me a ride along with them to Solvang, where there was rumored to be an underground pharmacy still stocking the medicine Uncle Rory needed. Word on the street told of a supply line that ran on and off safe-ish regions on Interstate 5; my brother said he heard from his medic colleagues at a makeshift hospital in Ashland that a loose network of underground-railroad-ish folks operating out of the rubble of what was once Portland were working to move medical supplies and patients in critical condition up and down the corridor. My brother, once a resident in urology in San Diego, had been drafted by the opposition to the front lines of that corridor. Only occasionally did we hear from him, and the news was grim. Seattle was where the organized rebellion started, and Obama was not letting a single part of the Pacific Northwest go unscathed. The Seattle area was also where my infirm Jewish uncle Rory was being hidden by sympathizers in one of the last standing outposts, in Snoqualmie at the base of Mt. Si. With the well-stocked hospitals from San Francisco to Seattle firmly held by Obama's forces, we were Rory's only hope. Both of Rory's sons in Seattle, one a photographer and one an outspoken journalist for The Stranger, disappeared even before my father did, but we were hopeful that the left-leaning network of Google and Amazon employees, who were the first to sense the shift in the wind as the internet began to go dark, squirreled them away across the border to Vancouver before Canada forcibly closed all its borders to fleeing Americans.

*

Now that I think of it, we shouldn't have been surprised by the visit to the ranch from a government tank. Government forces of course knew that my cousin Cliff was in the Navy before becoming an engineer for a private company. They knew he worked on submarines. Defectors who could have been of use to the government, who had pledged explicit allegiance to the government, were punished doubly. They weren't about to let Cliff's children survive. My mother tried to hide Penelope and Brian in the pale yellow storage unit near the goat pasture where we stored my late grandmother's things. It didn't take the soldiers long to figure out where the children were crouching, in the mouse shit between big plastic tubs of memorabilia scribbled on with permanent marker. In spite of the tank's size, my mother lunged in front of it and they cut her down so completely that I would later barely find a mangled limb to bury. The yellow-blistered bodies of Penelope and Brian were paraded on top of the tank in Los

Alamos that evening, evidence of what would happen to traitors, to government traitors, to their families. I wasn't there when they filled the storage unit with nerve gas, because other soldiers had discovered me down in the creek bed, trying to help hide the people camped in tents down there. I only glimpsed the yellow pallor of the children's skin from the clearing where the soldiers held me down as the tank rolled past, and I never heard them gagging or saw the muscle jerks that spread to take the breath from them.

I don't think I was supposed to survive, but one of the people hiding in the creek bed waited until nightfall and brought me to an old wine tasting room used as an elementary field hospital. I won't go into what the government soldiers did with me. I am a twenty-eight-year-old woman. I am a woman, period, and it happens to any woman here. It happens to women cornered by "rebel" forces, also. The better kind of rebels were able, a week later -- a week too late -- to regain Foxen Canyon. It's been weeks since they brought me home, but I still struggle to sleep and struggle to get up, too, watching the flicks in my vision animate the ceiling of the barn loft, where they've put a cot for me. I try to remember when I would look at Penelope and Brian and imagine having children, when I went home with cute UCSB students after dancing at a club all night because I liked having a body. Now all I do is hear the voice of my mother, humming the Fur Child song to Penelope and Brian, and their murmurs to her. Rebels walk outside, gravel crunching under their feet. I lie here in my cot in the barn loft and watch a nimble daddy-long-legs spider craft a large web in the shadowy corner, where wood meets wood.

Dispatch # 5

~Sent August 15th, 2013

Extract: transcript of interview/chat with Abu Faisal and Dr. Mahrouz
In Reyhanli (on the Turkey-Syria Border)
Recorded July 2013

Abu Faisal: There was boy selling coffee in Aleppo a few weeks ago. In a liberated area. A guy asked for a free cup of coffee, and the boy said, 'If the prophet himself came down and gave you credit I still wouldn't give you coffee.' If you know people from Aleppo it's not a big deal in Aleppo. It's something that Hababi would say in Aleppo. But the guy was not down with it at all. He said, 'You're an apostate, you're speaking against the prophet,' beat him; grabbed him from his coffee stand, brought him into the car, came back with a few bearded guys and shot him in the square and killed him. And then the three guys who did it fled. Then BBC comes along and says it's an Islamic militia taking over Syria, and it's the rebels and it's the FSA that did it. So the FSA rebels come and say, 'We didn't do this.' Well who did do it, and it's like--remember when I told you when a town is liberated, it's not really liberated? You still have SS jets flying over your head. You still have random thugs coming along. It's liberated but it's not. The government is gone, the FSA is there trying to fight the government, and in the meantime you have this vacuum. Who's gonna police the people? Who's gonna turn the electricity on? Who's gonna turn the water on? You know what I mean? That's all up in the air. So what Mahrouz is trying to say is that in the English media where he is, everyone's focusing on a story like that, which deserves its own focus, all right? But, they're forgetting that every day, one hundred to a hundred and ten people are killed in Syria. With an average since January of ten children a day.

Mahrouz: The people who is really being killed, nobody knows how many. Really nobody knows. How many people like Mohamed [the amputee downstairs] nobody knows. A lot of people die in silence and nobody knows anything about it...I'm sure you cannot change Barack Obama's mind. He's doing everything so *slow*ly like--

Abu Faisal: He can do it. He has access to direct phone. Atomic phone. Nuclear phone. In the international scene there's two sides to the conflict. On the SS side is Russia, Iran, Hezbollah, and Iraq. Iraqi government is with Assad.

Mahrouz: Under the table.

Ming: I even heard North Korea? And China's involved?

Abu Faisal: North Korea is North Korea. North Korea doesn't count. China doesn't ship anything either. They use their veto at the UN but they don't ship weapons. Russia, material support. Iran, material physical support. China's more vocal or whatever, just posturing against the US, it's nothing, it's, you know, political...wordsmanship? Is that what they call it?

Mahrouz: Barack Obama—I'm sure they know what's going on. And I believe, this guy, he is coward. He's...but the Democrats like, they sent the news to use cruise missiles, but this guy, he's a coward. An absolute coward. And he's not willing to go into history book in any way. Not a good way or a bad way. He just need to be like –

Abu Faisal: He won the Nobel prize, for –

Mahrouz: They give him the prize, and – preemptive strike from the nobel committee, actually, just to encourage him to use his, him being black, whatever, him being lawyer, whatever, something, and he's useless. Completely useless. It's a waste of time, his Presidency. It's absolutely a waste of time.

It's really a shame because it's absolutely rubbish waste of time. He's a nice guy. Very articulated. He articulate his speech very well. I heard him speak in –

Abu Faisal: Come on, we all fell for it. Hope and change and hope and change.

Ming: The problem with Obama was that he managed to be every person's hero, and so everyone was going to be disappointed. Because you could sort of impose anything you wanted onto him. Like everyone who voted for him thought, yeah, that's what he's about –

Abu Faisal: He's going to change *my* life...

Ming: Yeah. And so I knew that everybody was going to be disappointed but I didn't think that the NSA stuff would be under his watch, like, knowingly, and I didn't think –

Abu Faisal: Drone wars –

Ming: Yeah, I didn't think he would do *that*.

Mahrouz: I'm sure Syria is a small part of his business. And I'm sure –

Abu Faisal: The US does not—Syria's not strategic to the US. We know this.

Ming: Dude it is too!

Mahrouz: We're talking about human lives.

Abu Faisal: When Europe, you're the commander in chief and you're looking at planet earth or whatever like that, Syria, started off like this and now it's like this.

Ming: It'll grow into a 30 years war and then it *will* be our business!

Abu Faisal: That's what we're trying to — but he doesn't wanna — on *his* watch. We're telling him you have a chance to stop it, you have a chance to be on the right side on *your* watch...

Ming: Does he now, though? He had the chance two years ago and he didn't.

Abu Faisal: He can — listen. Remember when you asked what if everything stopped today what would it look like? It's a very messy it's very everything — but he can still, like, he's announced already the announcement that he's gonna arm and everything, and, da da da, we'll see if he follows it up. But like Mahrouz was saying or like I was saying earlier, of he just threatened, just threatened--or if he sent a couple missiles from all the way in the Mediterranean, from some aircraft carrier or whatever over Bashar Assad's house, he would have crapped himself. I mean, look at Israel. They bombed Syria three times so far. All right? They the they completely shat on Obama's theory and the army's theory that, 'Oh, Syria has these sophisticated air defenses and we can't go in, and it's not like Libya and it's so much more sophisticated than Libya.' And Israel's buzzing Assad's *house*. Like drinking martinis while they're buzzing him...Israel's sending a message to the US being like, like, we can do this, you know what I mean? We can do this using US weapons...

Mahrouz: Look, I have two brothers involved in this business and I'm scared to death about them on a daily basis. On the one hand I see shelling every day and I don't care. But on the other hand we say somebody needs to do this business.

Abu Faisal: He's talking about his brothers in Maarat. One is head of the hospital, one is head of the army.

Mahrouz: It's a dirty business, but somebody needs to do it.

(Pause)

Mahrouz: It's difficult – myself I mean honestly, how long do I not do exercise? Two months? Every day Skype meetings, meetings at hospital, Skype meeting with people at OSSUM. Sykpe meetings with these people here, with medical, with whatever humanitarian group whatever. Calls to this, to Abu Faisal, to this, to that, to get something. Its absolutely awful...Guys there is no economy, people dying, you let the war with generations of Syrians, three years without school, I promise you, you will get hundreds of thousands of kids will be easy to be criminals, to be drug dealer, on the street, whatever –

Abu Faisal: A lost generation, you know? I was telling you his brother finally had to move his kids out because they lost two years of school.

Ming: But, okay, so, again: if everything went the way you would have it go, what would that look like?

(pause)

Mahrouz: Look, if the regime down, the way like Qadaffi, the rebel managed to defeat the regime in that way, the country would be in mayhem for I don't how know long. But if the regime falls in organized way, watched by America, this is will be good way. My feeling is the United States can...arm the rebels from one side to push the regime back, put pressure on Russia, and tell them: this is serious business, we need to finish, needs to stop now, and they are not willing to stop it – if the United States wants to stop it they will stop it. Nobody will tell me Russia will stand firm, or whatever – Russia wouldn't stand firm. Russia *look* firm, because you are jelly and you are *let* them stand firm. But if...you need them just to give way, they will give way. I don't like the regime to fall like mayhem in the country and the killing would be huge.

Abu Faisal: There'd be a million problems, I mean — civil structure, everything, passports gonna be useless...
Mahrouz: I'd like the army to say, the intelligence service to say: change the aim of the secret service, change the top command and go and tell them, 'Guys, you are here to serve the people rather than kill them and the rest'...and keep the army and the police force whatever, 'Guys, you are here to look after the people'...and keep some element which is from the regime, Alawheen or whatever sect, Christian I think there is Christian in the opposition, to be like, not security like I could, talk for this minority of whatever. There's minority living in Syria for thousands of years never had a problem. Why is Christian becoming afraid from majority Sunni? For two thousand years nobody harmed them. And the Christians in Syria, forty years ago when Bashar's father come to power, used to be 50% of the population, now it is less than 10%...then the Christian in Syria go out, we lost our Jewish minority, we have 100,000 Syrian Jewish in Brooklyn alone.

Abu Faisal: They went here at the turn of the century.

Mahrouz: Ninety thousand Syrian Arab Jewish living in Brooklyn, New York. They run very good business. Who get them out of Syria? Muslims? Mayan emporer? Ottoman emporer? Who kicked them out of syria? Assad! This son of bitch—for the last forty years--after 1967. Who has a problem with Jews? I don't have a problem with Jews. I have a problem with somebody who kill my family, regardless...Assad says, "I'll be a hero and control the people for the next forty years because I've done good job."

Abu Faisal: There's no more Syrians troops along the border with Israel...the safest border Israel has is with Syria. It's the safest border. There are more attacks from Jordan, from Lebanon, from Egypt, but from Syria – if I were to run to a border and throw a rock at Israel, I would be shot by a Syrian soldier before I was shot by an Israeli. Assad doesn't want it. He knows that he doesn't want to get into a war with them, he's got some kind of deal, under the table...[they begin to talk about Hafiz handing the presidency to his son; recorder didn't catch it all:] ...We all believed it too in the beginning; we were like, 'This guy [Assad]'s gonna be a reformer.' He opens the economy – but only to his cousins, his family.

Mahrouz: Ming, I've been with him for six months eating, drinking, playing cars, with Bashar, in military court, 1980.

Abu Faisal: He's an ophthalmologist.

Mahrouz: How can she come here and not know he's an ophthalmologist?

Ming: I don't know anything. I'm not a journalist. I studied literary arts. I'm not trained in the ways of journalism.

Abu Faisal: That's fine; I just introduce you as a journalist because it makes it easier.

Mahrouz: Trust me if I had a hundred sheep, I wouldn't give it to Bashar to look after. Because he's useless.

Ming: They said the same thing about Bush. A guy who went to college with him said he couldn't run a convenience store.

Abu Faisal: He's clueless. Listen to his claim to fame over the last few years: 'I brought the internet to Syria.' I'm not kidding you. He says this to everybody. 'What did you do for Syria?' 'I brought the internet.' As if it was *his* to give. Remember how I was telling you how the government looks at us? 'You are there, I am here. I will give to you whatever I want. Don't question me, don't be smart. Remember I told you how only in Syria it means a bad thing, smart: it's the talk-backness.

Mahrouz: 1992 I've been kept in the army by the air force. He said we don't need anybody to be clever in this country. (chuckles)

Abu Faisal: When he was arrested that's what they told him.
Mahrouz: They told me we don't need anybody to be clever, you listen to us, you hear what we say, you do what we like, otherwise –

[The brother of Mahrouz, who is the leader of the FSA brigade for Maarat, comes in; our chat ends]

Dispatch # 6

~Sent August 22ⁿᵈ, 2013

Hello all,

In light of yesterday's events, I interrupt your regular dispatch series to bring in a "guest speaker": Abu Faisal, the Syrian man in his early thirties who lives abroad but returns and does aid work in Syria. He is the reason I was able to make my way over the border into Syria to the Atmeh refugee camp.

Atrocities occur daily in Syria, but this one was of such epic proportion that my main reaction is to shut up and listen. Bearing witness is something I've come to believe more and more is a serious business central to my understanding of faith, and it's not just watching. It's listening, too. So I wrote to the Syrian I know best to ask him for his perspective on the worst chemical weapons attack in recent history. I will resume with the next dispatch. Until then, here's most of the email he sent (edited for grammar and certain details so Abu Faisal can retain a smidgeon of anonymity). You may not share his views, but I think his perspective is a valuable one that he articulates powerfully, so I asked him if I could share this. Thank you all for listening, too.

--Ming

Hi Ming,

The US gov't know's exactly who did, how they did it and why they did it. To think otherwise is unimaginable.

Who: Assad.

How: Via rockets utilizing one of the world's (I'm not exaggerating) largest stockpiles of weaponized chemicals. That assessment is from the US gov't, not me.

Why: Assad is losing a lot of ground in the Eastern Ghouta area of Damascus. In the last month he's lost about 4 major neighborhoods to the FSA (most of whom are actual FSA, not Islamic extremists). That is a BIG deal to the Assad regime. Eastern Ghouta is the gateway to Damascus. It is the only way "in", strategically speaking, from a military perspective, to the city itself. Assad has used chemical weapons on a very small scale in Eastern Ghouta for many months now (check out the *Le Monde* story on this by two french journalists who lived there for a few months and came back with samples of Sarin which were confirmed by France, UK & US). These small scale chemical attacks failed to push back the FSA; it instilled massive fear in them (which was probably the main purpose) but it did not dislodge them.

So Assad pulled out his trump card. He's losing in Daraa and Dier Al Zor. He's pretty much lost most of Idleb and Aleppo. Raqqa is almost all lost. The suburbs of Hama are being lost. And the most extreme elements of Al Qaida are leading an offensive on his home state of Lattakia. Combine this with the events I described happening in Eastern Ghouta and this gives him every reason to use chemical weapons.

Why would Assad "be stupid enough" (as many so-called 'experts' are asking) to launch this attack when UN chemical weapons inspectors are in Damascus, not 15min away from the site of yesterdays massacre? It's quite simple. It's because he can. He has not only successfully called every bluff the international community gave him (100,000 dead souls can testify to this). But he has also successfully instilled (along with world governments) a (false) shadow of a doubt in every massacre he has perpetrated since March 15, 2011. The second reason means nothing to governments, they know the real deal, they know it's him. But it's important for the so-called 'media war' – which Assad has won hands-down.

The media want a photo of Assad pressing the big red button clearly labelled "Chemical Attack". Otherwise they will say "allegedly" and instill doubt in their audience. Well did Hitler 'allegedly' gas millions of Jews? Was there a photo of him pulling the lever? Did Pol Pot "allegedly" create his killing fields? Did Karadizc "allegedly" massacre 8,000 men and boys in Bosnia? Did Hutus "allegedly" massacre millions of Tutsis in Rwanda? and so on ... ad nauseum.

Placing this 'shadow of a doubt' over every atrocity leads to media "pussy-footing" (I can't believe i just used that word) around what is by any measure an actual slow-motion genocide. By far the largest of the Information Age. Using words such as 'alleged' or 'supposed' or 'unverified' or whatever, gives the guilty reader a way out, a way to relieve them of any guilt or need to actually do anything other than switch the channel or turn the page. In the West people are taught to not place guilt on anyone if there is any thought that is 'beyond the shadow of a doubt' that the person may not have committed the crime.

I have long ago lost the will to debate with people on "Why Assad would ..." or "How do you know the rebels did not ..." arguments. This is when I decided to start and focus on this small aid work since I realized that no one else will help us except ourselves, so I stopped waiting for Superman to arrive and save the day, but I still have a slight sliver of hope he may show up. If I play this game of debate-each-massacre with everyone, it means that Assad has already won. He successfully drowned every massacre since the beginning of the revolution in "doubt" even though there are thousands of videos and eye-witness testimonies confirming genocide. However, we live in a world were it will always be "alleged" unless the White Man says otherwise. It was only hours after this most recent massacre, the Chemical Attack, when people started forgetting about the 1,500+ dead human beings, the small children and babies slowly, agonizingly dying on camera and turned this grim episode in human history into a morbid academic debate on How, Why and Who. Not on "What can we do stop this?"

The governments of the world have only been too happy to have this "shadow of a doubt" card to play. It' lets them off the hook. It's the reason why Al Qaida is getting stronger by the day in Syria. "We won't arm the FSA since the weapons may goto Al Qaida" was the story used when there was barely an FSA and no Al Qaida. This policy not only gave birth to Al Qaida in Syria, but it made them flourish beyond their (AQ's) wildest dreams. For AQ, Syria is (literally) a Godsend. It [also] allowed Assad to make real his self-fullfilling prophecy of the "we are battling terrorists" line.

The media and some world governments have even side-stepped the human loss of life all together, not even addressing it and jumped straight into "The FSA bombed themselves with chemical weapons for world sympathy" story. The fact that supposedly educated people would even contemplate this much less propagate this "narrative"? If I debate this issue with "them" then they already won. The massacre is forgotten and we've already gone academic.

If the FSA had rockets enabled with chemical warheads, do you think for a split second that Israel or the USA would stand for that? Or even Russia? Obama's drones can spot me typing this email to you (and the NSA has surely had a field day with this email) you think they can't spot FSA fighters preparing highly sophisticated (weaponizing then launching a rocket like this is no easy task) and deadly rockets? Of course they can! If the FSA had these weapons then the US or more likely Israel would have destroyed them long ago. If Israel can blow up Assad's secret, well guarded bunkers full of missiles, they'll do the same for much less sophisticated FSA stockpiles should they exist.

The people of Syria have long ago stopped searching for sympathy from the rest of the world. The bucket of tears they desperately tried to collect from the rest of the world after each massacre is bone dry. To even debate this insane assumption (above) is beyond me. It's worth noting that every single atrocity or crime committed by the FSA or AQ in Syria was immediately addressed by the FSA themselves (meaning they admitted it and condemned it) and those that support the revolution were the first to highlight these crimes and condemn it. As for Assad and his supporters? They have denied every single innocent death they have committed over the last 40 years. Every single one. Without exception.

Show the world that our blood runs as red as theirs. That our parents cry the same tears that every other parent on Earth does when their child is lost. That we too enjoy life, that we laugh and joke and have the same dreams as any other person on Earth would have for a beautiful life. There is no use in "focusing" on any one event such as this massacre. In today's world, people forget in an instant and look for any excuse to do so.

When the first protesters where shot in cold blood on the streets in Daraa, I cried. Then the massacres started and I stopped crying or even shedding tears. 2+ years later I shed no tears. Yesterday when watching countless children on youtube struggling to breathe then die on camera, I shed no tears, I was mortified, angry, depressed and everything else. But I did not cry, nor did I feel like doing so. Nor was I shocked. I realized that I accepted what happened as "normal" as in, "This is what Assad does, this is what he always does and will always do," and that for the most part, the rest of the world agreed with me. My (non-Syrian) friends said, "Man, that sucked what happened in Syria, it's a shitty situation, man." And that was it. 1,500 people gassed to death has been reduced to a "shitty situation" that "sucks."

My point being is, people, my own friends, don't look at Syrians as humans anymore. We are numbers. This is not totally their own fault either. My Iraqi friends know exactly how I feel, but they are all tapped out of sympathy which I cannot blame them for. My Palestinian friends know how I feel and how Syrians feel more than anyone else, they respond "get used to it, this is going to last a very long time." Not in a cynical way, mind you, but in a way that is truly trying to comfort us (Syrians). Explaining to us that no one will help, stop getting our hopes up, stop dreaming, move on with life and expect nothing from anyone. The sooner we do that, the easier it will be to carry on with life.

However, we Syrians need that sympathy. What use is the food basket I prepare for a family to eat if they are gassed to death the next day? What use is the bakery we built if there are no people left to eat its bread? What use is a prosthetic limb placed on a person if he is killed the next day? We need support. We need government support. We cannot do this alone. If we do this alone then what you see today will go on for decades...

I can't do anything for the dead in Eastern Ghouta. What I can do is continue doing what I was working on the day before yesterday. Getting medical containers into Syria. Finding prosthetic limbs for amputees. Finding more flour for our bakery. Helping a man get a generator to re-start his business. Calling charities across America and Europe and begging them to give us a free ambulance. That is what I can do and what I will keep on doing. Even if the world watches every last Syrian die, because that is all I am able to do. We can't focus on 'events'; we need to stay focused on the bigger picture of a free and peaceful Syria.

Ahem. A word or two about two words: "activist" and "American".

I have trouble with the term "activist" the way I have trouble with the term "feminist". Calling myself those things seems to give those in official positions the permission not to take what I have to say seriously. Oh, look, another bleeding heart. Another angry activist. The terms carry a cultural connotation of humorlessness, when anyone who knows me can attest to how much I like to laugh. (Q: "How many feminists does it take to screw in a light bulb?" A: "That's not funny.")

And if feminism is, as Kramarae famously put it, "The radical notion that women are people," then the "activism" I enact with things like the trip to Turkey and Syria is the radical notion that *people* are people.

I couchsurfed with a lovely Turkish family during my first few days in Istanbul as June drew to a close. I slept in the bedroom of the thirteen-year-old daughter, whose walls were plastered with posters of Justin Bieber. No one in the family spoke English and I don't speak Turkish, but Mert, the twenty-year-old son, spent a year studying in Mexico, so he and I got along famously in Spanish. He was 19 when he studied abroad, the first-ever Turk at his school in Mexico. At that age I had been one of two Americans in the entire city of Syktyvkar, Russia, where I was spending time off from college working as an independent contractor/editor for a sustainable forestry foundation. That isolation, Mert and I agreed, is what taught both of us what makes people people.

Mert is a goofball and very social, which qualities led to the first Syrians I met in Istanbul. On one of my first days in the city, Mert took me to Taksim, wherefrom, between the day I started my Kickstarter campaign to come to Turkey and the day that campaign ended, protests had been broadcast the world over as Erdogan's police forces used tear gas and water cannons against protesters who didn't want their last city park, the Gezi Park there in Taksim, to turn into a strip mall.

Evening was falling, and the glints and noise from shopfronts, the roasted chestnuts for sale and bell-ringing ice cream salesman, the fake-flower-wreaths, all blended together in those million sonic and visual events that make a city center at night. Taksim was once again its usual busy-bee self, and that night there were no policemen that I could see. I stood where the Standing Man stood: where a man was arrested for standing still in Taksim near the end of the first substantial spate of protests and crackdowns. I already had plans to meet Abu Faisal and co. near the border in Reyhanli in a few days, but I wondered if there were a way to find Syrians here in Istanbul.

"Let's ask," said Mert simply. "Look, she looks as though she may be from Syria!"

And he marched over to a girl in a head scarf who was sitting outside of a makeup store, waiting on a friend. She wasn't from Syria; she and her friend were from Cairo. They walked with us for a few blocks, chatting about the 'youth in sustainable business management' conference they were part of. I was delighted that these two Egyptian girls were studying biomedical engineering. Women in the sciences are heroes, in my opinion, and in the 'Arab world' even more so. I have wondered, in the two months since, if she and her friend are all right.

"There are some Syrians in our hostel," one said as we parted ways.

"Can I give you my contact information in case any of them would like to talk?" I asked.

And that's how an email arrived in my inbox the next day from a man I'll call Mohamed. "I'm happy to chat," he wrote, "but I'm not sure whether it will be helpful because I am not an activist."

Something told me this young man had a lot to say, but wasn't going to say it in emails. I thought to myself there was no way I'd miss meeting him, then wondered if I had just watched too many Matt Damon movies and that's why I was assuming that this person wanted very much to meet and had a lot to say. By then I had moved from Mert's into a hostel near Taksim, so as to be near to the city center for interview opportunities. As I wended my way through the blue-lit late-evening in high summer, looking for the Starbucks, I thought to myself how often people the world over had arranged to meet at a Starbucks. Friends to study together. Semi-informal job interviews. A man and a woman in an Okcupid date. (Hell, a woman and a woman on an Okcupid date.) How often had what happened then happened elsewhere—my waiting at the wrong damn Starbucks. An American woman interested in the plight of Syrian people leaving a thin, bespectacled young Syrian man waiting at the *other* Starbucks.

There were panes of gold lit every which way at that hour, with the last gilded sunlight slashing those bars right up in store window displays, watch stores, restaurant signs: it felt like there were bits of gold everywhere. I squinted and scanned the street for this other Starbucks. A gold glint: spectacles. There he was. A thin, gentle, quiet young man of twenty years and his friend, a portly Syrian with spectacles too. I apologized for keeping them waiting, and we climbed to a quiet table away from other people on the third floor, where there was some semblance of silence. It was only after I had expressed grave concern over the human rights violations in Syria, including the chemical weapons attack that had happened earlier that month (August wasn't the first time Syrians died from nerve gas), and deep regret that America hadn't stepped in more forcefully, that the quiet Mohamed began to speak. "If the world thought Syrians were humans," he said quietly, "something would have happened, someone would have helped. Yes, over a hundred people died from chemical weapons. But for months, in Syria, that many people have died every *day*. Someone need to help the opposition, because Assad will kill us all before he stops."

"If someone does help, now," said Mohamed's friend, "it won't be because they think we are people, that we're humans

48

who don't deserve to be murdered. We know better than that now."

I sat across from them, two kids in my age group who were studying computers, hoping they would move from the hostel into a dorm room soon, hoping they'd be allowed to study where shells weren't falling. And they symbolize why I support my President in his decision to go it alone in Syria if he must. It's my first time supporting a US military strike. And I'm not a blind supporter of this man; the fact that the NSA got away with what it has under his leadership leaves me immensely ticked at him. It's a strange moment for me. I was against the invasion of Iraq and if I'd been alive during Vietnam, I would have protested against those actions also. I'm an obvious liberal: a bisexual democrat with a marked interest in the concept and practice of sustainability who went to elementary school where we said the Earth Prayer in sign language to a flag with our planet on it. The daughter of a retired Jew and a retired Episcopalian, I grew up on a hundred-acre ranch without church and went to high school an another ranch nearby, living in cabins and chopping wood to build fires to heat shower water. The people protesting against "getting involved" in the Middle East, in t shirts and with beards or beaded jewelry, look, in the photos I see of them on my computer here across the world, like the people in the village who raised me, the people in my parents' book club.

In the days since my last dispatch, one guest-written by the Syrian I call Abu Faisal, the interwebs have blown up with all sorts of opinions on Syria and a lot of blind spots on all sides of the arguments. I can offer nothing but another one of those, but my particular concern is with the clusterfuckitude of the situation we're in. My definition of a clusterfuck is when there is no way to help without causing some other disturbance, no way to affect an outcome without accepting some very strange bedfellows and enabling some of what we hope to stop...it's when there's no clear leader, but rather the cobweb of corruption and violence and abuse of power that can rush into a power vacuum-- a centuries-old tapestry of

49

grievances, vengeance and righteousness, crosshairs of competing beliefs that boil down to a basic difference in attitudes toward human existence and its purpose (not to mention the existence of nation-states and *their* purpose). People will die in Syria if we don't do anything. They'll die if we do.

If Obama had an attractive, unanimously supported option anywhere along up in here since Spring 2011, he would have taken it. It's been written lately that Syria truly is the problem from hell, from a foreign policy standpoint; it's the quintessential 'damned if you do, damned if you don't' scenario. People did not begin dying heinous deaths for unjust reasons on August 21st, 2013. They were killed in cold blood and broad daylight for protesting for democracy beginning in Spring 2011. When no one came to help the way Syrians were initially sure they would--"we're protesting for democracy against a dictatorship; America will help us—he's killing us, they're going to come help, they won't just stand by and let him do this--" but we did, and then extremists rushed in to fill the power vacuum. And now, black-and-white thinkers like the trolls I've heard from on Twitter recently tell me I'm interested in supporting Al Quaida and human heart-eating because I support military intervention on behalf of the 100,000+ Syrians who have died in a war that began as a protest fueled by the same hope that ran in the veins of the men who founded America.

I am a development worker. For the last twelve years, I spent about half the time I wasn't in school in the developing world. I originally was more suspicious than not of the American legal system, and I wore 'hippie clothes' and other visual markers of my disbelief in the credibility of my government. Then I realized, as I advocated for a Chinese dissident writer at the UNHCR in Mongolia, as I worked with refugee women from Congo, that my government and armed forces were why I was not shot in the head for going to school. Why I could practice the art I so desperately needed to express. Why I could fall in love with and date a black man or a woman if I so chose. So I went to school, I practiced art, and when I had the chance, I worked in Ecuador. Mongolia. Bolivia. Kenya. Russia. China. I didn't do so because I found American culture to be either perfect or empty, or American government to be either completely corrupt or flawless. I did it because I mean to treat the humans I meet and work with abroad like they have a birthright to life, liberty, and the pursuit of happiness. When I do this successfully, I understand it to be the most American work I do. I continue to believe this. It's what makes me a patriot. It's what makes me, practically speaking, with respect to my liberal upbringing in alternative communities, more conservative and moderate than I ever thought I'd be.

I was on a connecting flight in Khartoum, Sudan when I read on my phone about the Trayvon Martin verdict. I remember leaning my head against the window and staring at the tarmac in the pink light of dawn, wondering whether anyone had reason to listen to me. Abroad, innocent people were dying for democracy and we were doing little if anything to help them. At home, a black boy can be killed for breathing and being, and my legal system will sanction that. I believe what makes America great is its creed; at home and abroad, I knew, America wasn't living up to that creed. And that creed is why I presume to have something to offer the other human souls I work with in other nations. And it is a presumption; I have long since stopped trying to somehow separate development work (and the word "development", for that matter) from the presumption inherent in it. I only try to maintain a level of comfort with that I presume—that humans, and not just Americans, have a birthright to life, liberty, and the pursuit of happiness—and hope that any other presumption that comes along with it, with me, doesn't cause me to do more harm than good.

In June I heard, from someone working for a private security firm in Istanbul, that American secret service forces had been in Syria for months, quietly training Syrian civilians in the ways of managing and maintaining municipality in anticipation of the fall of the Assad regime. I hoped this was true. I had observed enough about Syria to realize the inevitability of human rights abuses that rush in when a legal system—however corrupt—is lifted away. Congo offers a similar lesson: I am no anarchist, because the absence of good governance is why Congolese women are much more likely to experience rape than not. Lawless lands are dog-eat-dog lands, roving thug-crew lands, and women and children are usually the first to fall in them, whether in Syria or Congo.

To those who contend that Syria "isn't our war", I simply would like to know what the criteria is for it *being* our war.

More than that, however, I'd like them to tell me how things would unfold if we continued *not* to intervene.

A megalomaniac has been indiscriminately killing his own people in more and more heinous ways for protesting for democracy, for well over two years. He is doing this in the Middle East, which is already destabilizing Lebanon, straining Jordan, and provoking Israel. He kept UN inspectors from the sites of chemical weapons attacks for days. A school was bombed in Syria yesterday with something like napalm. That a regional war swallowing those countries would affect us, I think, is indisputable. I'm not sure if what needs to happen is for one of these players to carry out an attack on American soil for us to realize that this doesn't just involve us philosophically as a nation that proclaims to be the greatest on earth due to the very creed we hesitate to defend, but involves us as mortal citizens on a planet that will never—can never--go back to isolationism. Mert and I have more in common than he does with many Turks his age, than I do with some of the kids back home who (and I don't begrudge them this) never left Santa Barbara. For better or for worse, *The Simpsons* and Starbucks unite me with a global group of young people in a system of interlocking societies and businesses that renders urbanity and access to the internet the top people-group-sorters and cultural literacy as the currency used in that triage. Mohamed studies computer science, and is waiting at the hostel for entrance to Turkish university. We both like lattes. If I get the chance to speak with Mohamed again, if he's still in Istanbul when I return in September, I will not tell him that his problem is not mine. I will tell him, as I did in June, that I am sorry reasons other than the right to human life were driving the forces that could have come to his aid.

It couldn't be clearer to Mohamed that Assad's people are not people to him. (Apparently, they are not people to Britain, either.) Assad shows no signs of stopping, and the scary extremists who rushed in and who are funding much of the opposition would not have been able to do those things-- rush in and fund – if leading nations had stepped in early on. But now both Assad *and*"anti-war" folks can point to the actions and views of those less-than-palatable extremists and say we're supporting them by stepping in. There are nutty extremists in the mix thanks to the two-plus-years of international inaction, but there are also vetted and fiercely secular FSA brigades like the ones who took care of me when I crossed into Syria's Atmeh refugee camp. They're kids, like me and Mohamed, carrying huge guns and wearing secondhand women's pink sorority t-shirts. They carry big guns because for two years Obama didn't carry a big stick the way they hoped he would. They carry guns because they're terrified, and their families are dead. They carry guns because they don't want the little orphans clustering outside the trailer door in the refugee camp to die too, and no one was helping them. The people and children I met in that camp just inside Syria, quiet and reserved and kind and intelligent, are who I hold in my mind when I read tweets about letting two enemies kill each other and not getting in the way of that. Dead toddlers are no one's enemy. The man who opened his tarp-tent the way he would have opened his nice door in Aleppo, who offered me tea and asked with concern whether I was comfortable when he saw me sweating, is not my enemy. If anyone is my enemy, the dictator who used the worldwide media to successfully dehumanize him is.

I have stamps on my passport because I believed that what makes America great is that many Americans are fortunate enough to be in a position to treat the downtrodden like they are people. The message leading nations gave Syrians is that they're not. Inaction is action, perhaps not for everyone, but for Obama, because our country's founding document, whatever its faults, is at heart a humanistic one. Not an American-istic one or a Western-istic one. Mohamed is a human. So are the babies who seized up, turned green, and foamed at the mouth as they suffocated to death on cement floors in Damascus ten days ago. So will the babies in Los Angeles, or New York, or Chicago, or Paris, or London be, if chemical weapons use is left unaddressed and our promises to people who wanted democracy and died for it go unfulfilled in the face of sociopathy on the nation-state level and slow-motion genocide. We will further lose our purpose as a world leader and the right to see ourselves as a beacon of freedom. So yes, I am a bleeding heart and an activist precisely because I am a patriot, and an interventionist in this case. We've used chemical weapons before, and our government bears the marks of corruption and the abuse of executive power. There are unjust things happening all over the world that we have turned a blind eye to, and proxy wars we have fought for hypocritical reasons, and democratically elected leaders our CIA helped to depose and assassinate. We are far from perfect.

But it was America the Syrians kept looking to. It was that name they shouted, not in hatred as they threw grenades but in grief as they held their dying brethren. I will not let a video of some crackpot eating a human brain or decapitating a priest cloud what I have to say to the gentle young man in a coffee shop about what he is worth. To the extent that I can prevent such a cloud from having me tell him he doesn't deserve what every human deserves, I can call myself American and be proud of it.

I couldn't understand what the people in the videos were saying as they held children who seized to death on

August 21st, as they tore off the babies' clothes and rinsed their wee bodies again and again with water, as they pumped the little chests and blew into the open, frozen mouths, and they gave up and held the babies to the cameras (cameras of people who would later die from CW exposure) like an offering as they shouted in agony. I didn't grow up with church, but the tone of what they cried as they held the tiny corpses did sound something along the lines of: why hast thou forsaken me.

Call me an activist, but this is why I set out on this journey: we will not forsake them on my watch. Or, *I* will do my best not to forsake them. Once again: I'd like the nay-sayers to tell me how things would unfold if we continued *not* to take action in Syria. And no one can answer me that.

Dispatch # 8
Sent September 4th, 2013

Dear Ones,

Once again, in keeping with the seriousness and immediacy of current Syria news, Abu Faisal is "guest-speaking". I know many of us have read the *Washington Post*'s "9 Things About Syria You Were Too Embarrassed To Ask". When I asked Abu Faisal for his take on the article, his answers and additions were not only characteristically observant and lively (who knew the anthem singer was a firefighter and not a cement mixer) but they also started me thinking about something I hadn't in all this, which was the act of reaching out to Assad's forces.

And once again, you may not agree with Abu Faisal, but I'm always glad for the chance to listen to a Syrian on these issues, and when things are moving as quickly and seriously as they are this week, I think it's important to give a Syrian the mike. I'll be back for Dispatch #9.

Yours,
Ming

September 2nd:

"I read that WaPo piece (actually glanced over it), I hate it when people say "The Assad regime is terrible BUT ...." and they go on to give you several, mostly unfounded reasons to do absolutely nothing. I warn you, I am not objective and will be biased. This does NOT mean that I will lie, embellish, or exaggerate, though. As a Syrian, we don't need to, since the reality is horrible enough, so much so that many people don't believe us.

1. What is Syria:

Fighting between government forces and rebels has killed more 100,000 and created 2 million refugees

I know the purpose of this article is for the "I don't have time to read 1,000 words about some Arabs" crowd. However, the generalization pushes the reader to believe that fighting between two equal parties (which is what most people believe a civil war is defined as) has led to the deaths of +100,000 people and led to the 2 million refugees.

For accuracy, you should check this site out. It is the Center for Documentation of Violations in Syria: http://www.vdc-sy.info/index.php/en/ ... it's a very thorough website and provides the most conservative estimates on the number of dead and missing in Syria since the revolution began. Just click on any of the tabs and press (submit) and you can see the number of dead in each category (ie, civilians, fighters, children, Assad regime soldiers). This site is the most stringent on fact-checking its numbers; this is why the number of dead is "only" about 75,000.
Most Syrians believe that is is maybe 200,000 or more. For every dead person documented on video and reported to activists networks, there are many more that are not reported or recorded; they are simply buried and forgotten.

This site is easier to navigate and is also very conservative. It's the one I use the most to cite: http://syrianshuhada.com/?lang=en& (it translates to "Syrian Martyrs). You can click on the links on the right to get very easy descriptions and statistics. It's run by the Syrian Revolution General Commission, one of the first activist networks to establish when the revolution began. They're count is 79,000 dead.

The number cited in the press of "100,000+" probably includes the numbers above, plus some for margin of error and about another 25,000 soldiers from the Assad regime that are not included in the above estimate since Assad does not disclose the number that died defending him.

Anyways, back to why I don't like Max Fisher's generalization. It's that the death toll is heavily heavily skewed towards dead civilians, most of whom (almost all) are killed by the Assad regime. There is no doubt, even by admission of Pro-Assad forces/supporters that the vast majority of dead on Assad's side are soldiers, not civilians. So no Max, 100,000 dead are not because of 'fighting in a civil war' ... it's because the Assad regime's military machine is attacking a civilian population that only decided to pick up arms after enduring 8 months of hell in peaceful protests. Assad has the unconditional support of entire nations. The rest of Syria has to smuggle weapons and bullets that cost $1 each. By and large, up until this day, most weapons that the FSA have in their possession are from capturing Assad's bases.

2. Why are people in Syria killing each other?

Again, Max starts off saying that we are "killing each-other". Even if we include all the death and misery from Al Qaida and extremists, statistically speaking (not that it matters to the dead anymore) we are still experiencing a mass-massacre – that is one-sided in nature – by the Assad regime. The FSA was created to STOP this. Not to attack. The first defectors would defend homes and neighborhoods, not attack. Not until the FSA became more organized and tens of thousands of non-military men join did they start attacking Assad bases to stop them from shelling/attacking them. It was a clear, simple and obvious survival tactic that any living organism would undertake to preserve their life.

First, security forces quietly killed activists. Then they started kidnapping, raping, torturing and killing activists and their family members, including a lot of children, dumping their mutilated bodies by the sides of roads.

Even before the revolution, nothing was done quietly. When Assad came for you, everyone would know about it. This is on purpose to deter anyone else from event thinking about opposing the regime. Now, onto the revolution, the young boys in Daraa who sparked this revolt were not arrested and tortured quietly either, hence why protests happened. Again, in Syria, nothing was done quietly. Just because a US newspaper did not report it does not mean we died quietly. *Then they started ..."* This also happened before the revolution and from the first days when it began, it was not something that "progressed". It was always there.

Just to give you one example, the father of one of my dad's friends was abducted, tortured then killed by the Assad regime about 15 years ago and was dumped, very publicly, in a garbage can on a road in Aleppo. These things happened in Syria more often that not ... but they also "never happened" because no one would ever speak about it or acknowledge it out of fear it would happen to them. Why was the man taken and killed like that 15 years ago? No one quite knows, they assume because he wrote a book or was about to that was slightly critical of the regime at the time. Of course, it could have been for anything.

" ... and now it looks like Assad is coming back"

I hate arguing this point since it's one that makes me look the most biased, but Assad is not "coming back". He has already been defeated. He leads his supporters/forces via proxy only thanks to massive Russian / Iranian / Iraqi / Hezbullah support. Assad can be called the strongest warlord in Syria now since he has planes, tanks, scuds and of course chemical weapons, but he is not coming back. He is losing on every "front" except for Homs. There is not a single exception to this.

3. That's horrible. But there are protests lots of places. How did it all go so wrong in Syria? And, please, just give me the short version.

Fair analysis until you get to the "Fareed Zakaria" stuff. Yes, Syria's borders are artificial, which is the same for all Arab nations and if you think about it, the same for every nation on Earth. I take exception to his very 'Orientalist' views of Arabs. That we, unlike other humans, are basically animals that need to be separated, lions and hyenas if you may, that cannot co-exist and will kill each-other unless a zookeeper keeps us in check with a stick (or gun) or should be separated for life. This "narrative" (buzz-word of the year so far) is the same one that was used by Arab dictators for the last half-century to 'keep us in check', saying that without a tyrant ruling over us, we would all turn to rabid animals and kill each other with anarchy and chaos ensuing.

Zakaria's " *.. inevitable re-balancing of power along ethnic and religious lines.*" argument holds no historical precedence. Not in Syria or the wider Arab world. His only example, Iraq, is a such a poor one that we cannot honestly take it seriously. Iraq was invaded, destroyed and divided by a super-power. Blaming today's violence in Iraq and in Syria on "ethnic re-balancing" shows a lack of very basic history on Arabia, which, by any measure, had the same ethnic, religious and cultural issues all nations on Earth historically had. We have been led to believe that this is only exclusive to us and is part of some "great, historic, 1,400 years in the making, epic Sunni - Shia battle royale!"

Arabia has been and still is a melting pot of cultures, religions and ethnicities. It was "born" this way and despite a century of imperialism then another half century of dictatorships (a parting gift from the imperialism) we still are, by and large, a peaceful melting pot. Our wars were no worse than others. Our issues no worse than anyone else's. The Levant area had no borders before (neither did the rest of Arabia for that matter). To imply that today we are witnessing

60

the "re-balancing of borders" fails to reconcile that fact (we were borderless before!!!).

In Syria specifically, if you ask any Sunni, Christian, Alawite, Druze or whatever how they felt about their neighbors before or right when the revolution broke out, none would have spoken ill of the other. Most Syrian Sunnis NEVER blamed the entire Alawite sect from benefiting from Assad. Quite the contrary, everyone in Syria knew that some of the poorest Syrians, apart from the Kurds, where Alawites in the mountains in Lattakia. Even today, many Alawite villages have no water or electricity or proper roads, very uneducated populations with no real jobs (this was purposely done by Assad to ensure that poor Alawites would work in the gov't or army, ie *for* him, and that they would *owe* him if he ever called on them to do something). Everyone in Syria knew this. Historically Alawites have alway been poor and yes, many were discriminated against for various periods of time, there is no hiding from that or glossing over it, but to blame that on the current revolution and resulting war is quite preposterous. No one is fighting today for what people did 100, 200, 300 or 1,000 years ago. It's an argument the West uses to place us in our nice little box and say "yes, that's the reason why this is so ..."

Also, many people assume Fareed is Arab (from his name) but he is not. Nor to my knowledge has he ever lived in Arabia.

4. I hear a lot about how Russia still loves Syria, though. And Iran, too. What's their deal?

I don't pretend to know what Russia's foreign policy is or why they do what they do, I can only assume. But what I do know is that this "great naval base" that Russia has in Syria is a crappy semi-port with some barges. Is it strategic to Russia? Maybe, you'd have to ask them. But it's not a reason why they are backing Assad. Reasons 2 and 3 probably explain most of why Russia is backing Assad, it's all 'super-power' politics,

Syria is a pawn, nothing more. and as for reason 4 ....
HAHAHAHAHAHAAHAHAH! REALLY! Max thinks Russia is
dependent financially on arm sales to Syria!!! That makes me
question his international reporting credentials. Syria owes
Russia so much money, before the revolution, it's probably one
of the reasons Assad gave Russia the 'naval base' port. Does
Max think Assad has been paying Russia for the endless
supply of arms, ammo, spare parts and supplies being sent the
last 2 years? And if so, where did this money to pay for them
come from? Syria does not function as a state anymore. There
is no real income for the regime, it's very negligible.

As for Iran's involvement, it's about maintaining its
influence in the Arab world. Iran's only real Arab ally is Assad
(formerly Syria). It needs to maintain that to support its
proxies in Lebanon (Hezbullah). Max is quite outdated to
think that Hamas is still getting support from Iran. Hamas is
linked to the Muslim Brotherhood which in turn hate Assad.
Hamas left Syria last year and sided with the revolution after
relocating from Damascus. Qatar filled in the support gap after
Iran stopped supporting Hamas. Hamas has even sent some
fighters to Syria to help the FSA.

5. This is all feeling really bleak and hopeless. Can we take a music break?

The singer in the video is George Wassouf, a very vocal
supporter of Assad. He's originally Syrian but has Lebanese
citizenship. He's also a coke addict (true story, I'm not just
hating).

The song Max cites, "Come on Bashar Leave", is the
anthem of the revolution. The composer was not a cement
mixer, he was a firefighter in Hama. The composer was killed
by Assad's forces for writing the song. His name is Ibrahim
Qashoush. He had his larynx ripped out of his throat and was
thrown into the Orontes River where he died. The Orontes
river in Arabic is the "Assi River" and means "disobedient"

since it's the only river in Syria(or maybe even the region) that flows south to north and all others flow north to south.

6. Why hasn't the United States fixed this yet?

I think I answered this before. Arming the FSA will not "ultimately empower jihadists". In fact, not arming the FSA is empowering them. I'm not on the ground fighting. I'm far from anything that even resembles a military-strategist wannabe, but I can tell you what I know and see. If the US strikes a few scud bases, some airports and puts on a meaningless fireworks display in other areas WITHOUT killing innocent civilians, then this will scare the shit out of the regime as the mere threat of a strike already has. Fear causes confusion and disarray. Couple this with arming the FSA, and Assad could be finished in 6-12 months. Does the US want this? No. They want a softer transfer of power. Only a dictator, by nature, does not transfer power. So the US must add a significant 3rd element to this plan ... REACH OUT TO ASSAD'S FORCES!   Give them a way out. Give them an alternative to the current "fight to the death for Assad". Give them guarantees for their safety from extremist Jihadis (who, when not chopping heads off, mostly are fighting Assad not because he's a tyrant, but because they think he and his tribe are infidels). Have Assad's forces hand over those that have blood on their hands (ordered massacres, executions ...etc). Help them ensure that no mass reprisals will take place. That no grand 'score-settling' for the past two years will take place. This can be done; the US has the contacts and ability to make it happen. I myself know at least one very high ranking former soldier who still maintains contacts with Assad soldiers just for this reason. Bottom line is, if I know this, then the US/NATO do too and they can act on it. Many Alawites would like to defect from Assad's army but can't. A military coup is needed to make this work and to ensure that whatever is left of the state can be preserved and revived back to life so a semi-

smooth transition can take place. As for the remaining, I think
I answered the rest of the questions above."

Dispatch #9
~Sent October 11ᵗʰ, 2013

There has been something keeping me from finishing this dispatch.

I was in Westgate mall in Nairobi, Kenya, typing up notes for this dispatch, in the week before the Al-Shabaab terrorists responded to the presence of Kenyan armed forces in Somalia by storming that mall and slaughtering innocent men, women, children, and babies. There was blood where I sat and typed, blood and screams everywhere, and the waitress I liked to chat with might be dead. But I wasn't there. (The surest way to survive and event, I suppose, is not to attend it.) Like how I was at the border crossing between Syria and Turkey earlier in the summer weeks before the chemical attack in Damascus and subsequent global attention not on the suffering of Syrian people as much as the political theater of what President Obama was going to do about it. That border crossing, Abu Faisal reports, is now closed for the most part. Over the weeks since we were there together, since we made that crossing and toured Atmeh refugee camp, it has become so dangerous that Turkey has clamped down on the crossing points once controlled by the FSA. Humanitarian aid is even harder to deliver, now that Assad's effectively been given the global go-ahead to continue slaughtering civilians with shells, with guns, with starve-outs, with everything but nerve gas. The FSA is fighting Assad *and* extremist jihadists, and that splintering between rebel forces will only become more pronounced. The secular members of the FSA are the ones whose families were killed for protesting peacefully for a more democratic government. The jihadist factions are there because Assad is, if you can believe it, too liberal and modern for them. He is, in their eyes, not a ruthless dictator slaughtering his own people but an apostate, and *that's* why he needs to be done away with.

Westgate's Israeli-owned cafe is the one the Al-Shabaab terrorists targeted. I would sit on its patio and order the grilled halloumi cheese salad, chatting with a waitress there who had very nicely groomed eyebrows about my work doing theater with Congolese refugee ladies in one of Nairobi's slums. I would put headphones in my ears and listen to the interviews I had recorded with Abu Faisal and Dr. Mahrouz, trying to type up Abu Faisal's hilarious summing-up of Thomas Friedman ("I think this! My moustache says this!") or Dr. Mahrouz talking shit about Assad's strange power plays with land and landmarks ("fucking bitch we don't need the lake!"), remembering the cups of strong, brown tea we drank together, and the mother of a young amputee who would serve them to us. Her son the amputee meant to return to Syria. He was the one who looked like my own childhood friend. I have photos of him standing on the prosthetic limbs that were made in the workshop downstairs. He was exceedingly proud, and I felt guilty that I did indeed register his presence more readily than when he had been wheeling around below eye level. There's no way he wouldn't have felt that: he was robbed of much more than his legs when he started being a subordinate thing noticed. I wonder if he's still alive.

At the border crossing near Atmeh, in Syria, had Assad's forces or jihadists attacked, as in the cafe in Westgate, my privilege would not have kept me alive; in fact, my blonde hair, blue eyes, pale skin, and lack of street smarts would probably have gotten me killed within the first minute. Instead, I flew to the United States on the 19th of September, two days before the mauling at the mall. I spent a weekend in the bay area of California with my cousins Cliff and Dorothy, and their children, who had not seized, defecated, suffocated, and foamed at the mouth until they were dead, but who had instead grown at least a half-inch each over the summer. I drove my used van Maizie, my first car, duct-taped across the top of the windshield and scraped on both sides, who I bought in Indiana last December and drove west after my masters coursework was done. She is dirty and her seats are folded down and we filled her with boxes and a set of drawers Cliff

66

and Dorothy were done with. I drove into North Berkeley to have lunch with my friend Linda, a 73 year old woman who had had lung surgery over the summer in a hospital that was not a school civilians had hastily redone to use the desks as makeshift hospital cots. Linda was sewn up by surgeons and picked up by friends, because she had surgeons who had gone to medical school and she had friends who were alive. We ate cheese and drank tea. I drove down the 101 in the sunshine, arriving at sunset at my new place, one which I hadn't seen in person. The small guest quarters of a big fancy house in the foothills of Santa Barbara. I share the apartment with another PhD, who was gone that evening, so I wandered the place alone, amazed that for the first time in over ten months I wouldn't be couchsurfing. I could see the stars. I could hear the crickets. I was less than an hour's drive from the ranch where I spent my childhood, where my parents brought me the day I was born, at the end of a September. I slept on a mattress my good friend had found off craigslist and unloaded into my empty room for me. I woke up at sunrise and when I parted the curtains, there were two baby deer across the way under the oaks. As I drove from the mountains to campus, which is literally on the beach, I burst out laughing. A school on the beach full of nice people and salt on the air, can it be? I remembered Nairobi. I remembered the Charles Wright poem "Black Zodiac": *What can we say to either of them? How can they be so dark and so clear at the same time?*

In my ears, Abu Faisal's letter, the one he sent after the chemical weapons attack outside of Damascus, rings like a bell: "The media and some world governments have even sidestepped the human loss of life all together, not even addressing it and jumped straight into "The FSA bombed themselves with chemical weapons for world sympathy" story. The fact that supposedly educated people would even contemplate this much less propagate this "narrative"? If I debate this issue with "them" then they already won. The massacre is forgotten and we've already gone academic."

It's a bit like talking to my friend Maureen, who was supposed to be on the United flight that was hijacked and flown into the World Trade Center but who decided to leave New York on September 10, 2001 instead. Like George Oppen before me, I cannot distinguish meaning from narrative. I think story is central to the human mind and the stories we hear and tell about the world are the way we make sense of it. I'm not sure how to give words on the meditative response humans have to such horrors that did not happen to them. It did not happen to me: there is nothing to say about it. Some people visited the World Trade Center as tourists on September 10th. Certainly the argument that time and space are illusions, that the human mind invents them, that they're malleable, could feel far away if one is in the place where children are gunned down and disemboweled, where schools are bombed. Assad has been given license to continue slaughtering civilians as long as it's not by gassing them. Kerry made a remark off the cuff that changed the course of the debate on and American strike in Syria. It was one news cycle, really. I watched Putin run circles around President Obama, manipulating and bullying like the presidency-is-reign shark he is, like President Obama's slightly smarter and less kind-hearted older brother.

I changed buses when I worked with the girls in Nairobi, which required being downtown in the gritty city part (where I was accordingly robbed twice by enterprising pickpockets) not in the lush part like Westgate. But there was a Hilton gym there and I would go through the metal detectors, hand the uniformed folks my backpack, and go up to where the pine smell of the sauna room would lull me into my remix of the emotional freedom technique, which I taught the girls in my theater group, who are all trauma victims. Touch the pressure points, and all the while recite the things that bring us back into the present. "My name is Ming Holden. I'm twenty-nine." Tap the temples. "I'm in Nairobi." Tap the cheeks and above the lips. "I have a place I can come and relax that I am grateful for." Touch the tips of your fingers with the other tips, and tap them together. "Today I worked with women who amaze me and whom I love, and they don't get to have these things, and I'm sad about that. It's September seventeenth, twenty thirteen..." And so on. Twice I got a massage from women who told me how they pray. One of them had lost two sons. There was tea outside the massage room. Chamomile. I kept the nondescript bag I'd brought into Syria at the gym in Nairobi, stuffed with the cheapest running shoes I could find after my old black ones floated away from me somewhere in Istanbul. I noticed their absence as I unpacked the big gray bag that Egypt Air lost for two days, the bag I had gone back to the airport to fetch in the international terminal, the one that caught fire less than two days later., the terminal's blaze making world headlines.

There in the locker room, in September, in Nairobi, I put black duct tape on the shoes I bought when, the next day, the velcro strips fell off in my hands. I'd run on an elliptical. I'd ask to change the channel to CNN. I watched the Syria drama unfold because that's what it was: political theater. I watched the brute deaths of innocents reduced to some moving rhetoric; I watched the drama unfold as two world leaders saw things in terms of justice and power, respectively, and the power-monger won in the short term. (Though I think we all know no chemical weapons would be leaving Syria right now without at least the threat of a US strike.) I accepted that words would always be so: that I'm doing something that isn't much different when I write to you all. I use language to move people because that's what speech is. It's a violent reduction of any uniqueness. It's usable to justify wars that aren't worth fighting and to avoid wars that are. It's malleable, and we can use it skate around difficult issues. After all, we don't sugar-coat things with sugar. I thought of the eyes of the men I saw at the checkpoint, some in military vests, holding guns near the crowds of children. Checking us through. I was entranced by the eyes of most of the Turkish and Syrian men I met without knowing why. Maybe it was the green eyes and olive skin.

There was only one pair of eyes I was sure I didn't like. As we got near to the place in the camp where Karam Foundation built a playground—the fence around it had been robbed by residents of the camp by that time — a car approached. It's wasn't a very nice car. The guy in the car had bad eyes. They were empty. He spoke briefly with Abu Faisal from within the car. Abu Faisal stood with his thumbs linked through the straps of his backpack.

"What was that?" I asked as the car pulled away.

"Nothing," Abu Faisal said. "Nothing to worry about."

I asked again, and again, he brushed me off. It's the only time he ever did so in the days we spent in Reyhanli and the day we spent in Syria, which is probably why it annoyed me so, and why I paid attention to it. At some point, Abu Faisal did explain a little more. The guy was doing his own patrol. He saw foreign people in the group, saw the chance to gain something. He patrolled not because anyone else wanted him to, but because he had decided it was his area. That, like the open sewage stream darkening the dust two feet outside the camp kitchen, where huge silver tureens cooked one meal a day for the camp's residents, is what happens in unplanned cities with no governance. That's what lack of infrastucture looks like: a river of shit and a pair of empty eyes.

There was a man in Atmeh, who asked Abu Faisal to translate and who looked at me in particular as the American in the group. He was a former police officer. "He's a says that he'd even want peace with Israel if it would stop Assad," said Abu Faisal. "He says the FSA needs help and protection from America—just some arms. They'd take care of the rest. They just need the weapons they can take down Assad with."

The young boy beside him said they were from Maarat Al Nouman, the village Abu Faisal's family friends hold on their shoulders by maintaining a hospital and bakery there and leading the local FSA brigade. The man, whose hair was silver and who wore what still looked to me like a long nightgown, shushed him and said they were from somewhere else. ("His view about Israel isn't popular at all," Abu Faisal explained later. "That's why he lied about where he's from.")

That day in Atmeh, dry and hot with rows of muted, dusty olive trees stretching into the hilly distance, the man, who defected from Assad's army, spoke with his hands as much as his voice, bringing them down for emphasis.

"He's saying the U.N. is asleep," said Abu Faisal. "We need America because the U.N. is sleeping."

*

I connected in Istanbul between Kenya and home. It happened to be where the cheapest flight combo had me pit stop, so I extended the pit stop for a day or two. A friend from Seattle was in town and we wandered the grand bazaar of shopkeeper harassment. We also wandered Topkapi palace, where rubies and emerald glittered from every display case. In the same Starbucks where we met initially, months before, I met again with Mohamed's friend, the portly, bespectacled Syrian who, like Abu Faisal and his cousin, didn't tell his family members that he'd gone back into Syria. His own parents are in Homs, but he still travels into Syria, into liberated areas, setting up satellite internet networks for people. "If the war has taught me one thing," he said that night in September, shaking his head, "it's that eighty percent of Syrians are bad people."

He described the men driving petrol out of Syria, where it was needed, for the money. They didn't like doing it, knew it was wrong, but had to feed their families. Maybe that's what war is. Maybe that's what it does to people. Despicable things are done and then the ones who are left do them too, turn into people they don't admire, to survive. A wave of hatred, outward, inward, rippling from a central disfunction. I turned 29 on September 30th, and it was my first day of PhD seminar. Theories of embodiment. We had to bring in a video or photo of something that would necessitate our giving undergraduate students a disclaimer. One person brought in a book of ballet dancers naked, embracing. One brought a clip of a performance artist who made himself bleed. One brought a clip of that documentary about the artist in China who pretended for a long time to tell the public that the human fetus he was eating was a real one. "There are no laws against cannibalism," he'd explained amiably to the interviewer.

I brought in footage two days old, a youtube clip from Raqqa, where a school had been bombed. As Eliot Higgins, an arms tracker who has watched thousands of videos of the warfare in Syria, put it, "that's bad, even for Syria". The disemboweled bodies loaded into a truck aren't recognizable as human. And yet, there is always the contingent of people who believe that this was, in fact, staged, as I explained to my graduate seminar. And we study performance, so let's pay attention to what convinces us. *We've already gone academic.* Let's talk about citizen journalism. My birthday came and went, new friends swam with me in the Pacific, I got sand in my hair and my car. I jogged up the mountain roads from where the fancy couple has their house and the guest quarters I live in. More and more opulent houses. I kept registering changes of temperature and the smells of different plants: a sudden keep of cold air near that smells like anise. Then a rush of heat, very dry heat, above the creekbed. I made it to the mouth of Rattlesnake Trial, sat on a rock with a top shaped like a dish that fit my body when I lay down and curled up in it like I was in the womb. I watched, sideways, as leaves fell in little gold bits down into the creekbed. I could hear the voices of other hikers. Humans were dying savage deaths, nowhere I could see. There's another pair of rocks above, that I would discover later among the blackened sagebrush that was left by a fire that scorched the area years back: those two rocks might actually be one rock. The shape is like that of two dolphins jumping, their front halves. Rocks are uncanny like that; they almost hang upwards in ways that would be impossible except that it's right there in front of you.

My professor explained a few things about Descartes and Ponty to me when I came into his office hours. He used an hourglass actors gave him after he directed a play at Harvard. This professor is exceedingly cheerful, Latino, and flaming. It's like having Hank Azaria's character in "The Birdcage" as a philosophy professor. I can't get enough of him. He explained phenomenology's attention to the process of getting to the point when we realize we're in a body, when we realize that we're thinking. After leaving his office I put on my duct-taped shoes, I aimed for a run around the lagoon right by the theater building, and got about fifty meters, and then the ocean was there. The shoes came off. I went in, slowly, level by level of cold banding my body. The breakers were a little relentless, but beyond them there was calm—suddenly deep water, the dark suggestions of kelp. I thought of the poem I wanted to write to my friend Labri about it, because we've exchanged poems for over a year now. The mountains beyond campus, which I could see from my spot in the water, were striped with vegetation. When we were little, a friend called them ice-cream mountains because the plant matter looked like chocolate syrup on the mountains from far away. I paddled, I did what I do when I try to meditate, and felt the swaying to and fro of my body being carried along by the sea. The sun hammered down, chinking the water with points of bright. I recited my name and the date to myself, wiggled my fingers and toes. The swaying was easy.

What was it like before you realized you were you? My professor had asked.

I remember the first moment I thought, 'I'm me,' I had answered.

And before that?

Nothing. I didn't know I was like other people. That inside of the people I saw were consciousnesses like mine: that I was in something that looked a lot like them. I didn't know I looked like a person. Being inside my on body was so different from looking at someone else's.

Easy, sway, kelp, calm.

Dispatch # 10
   ~ Sent November 29ᵗʰ, 2013

Dear Ones,

   Abu Faisal, who brought me over the border to Syria's Atmeh refugee camp in July, went back into Syria a few days ago and here is what he wrote to me about the situation on the ground out there now.

   On this holiday weekend I don't think some time spent considering the realities invoked in this account would be time wasted. We are all very fortunate, and have a lot to be grateful for. We probably all wish Syrians had more to be grateful for than they currently do. The least we can do, I believe, is not to turn a blind eye.

   There are so few reporters out there now that I value Abu Faisal's missives even more than ever, for the window they give us to a place the media is making it pretty easy to write off and forget.

Yours,
Ming

Hi Ming,

   Thanks for the kind words, got back a few days ago. Hope your PhD is going well!
   Situation is both horrible and hopeful, if that's possible, at the same time. It's horrible since little has changed since I last went in July - in terms of the humanitarian situation that is. Still very little aid getting to so few people. It's hopeful in

that the resolve of the people to overcome every hardship is still there, even though in some cases it's by just a thread.

I guess some major changes since my last trip is that Assad uses his warplanes far more than before, or at least during that last few times I went this year. As we headed to the town I was to stay in (Dr Mahrouz's home town), a Sukhoi-24 jet pounded the road just behind us. We were lucky that we were far enough in front to just keep going. When we got out of the car the jet circled again and hit a building at the other end of town. I mention the name of the jet only because, and according to my friends, this jet is far more advanced than the MiG jets Assad usually uses. Sukhoi's can hit from farther up and are more accurate (again, according to people in the town). The fact that Assad is using these jets more and more means that his maintenance (historically atrocious in the Syrian military) is getting better. This does not mean that Assad's soldiers are doing a better job maintaining the planes, but, in my humble opinion, it's that Russia is helping Assad much more than before. To keep a Sukhoi-24 jet in shape to bomb each and every single day is not easy, it's very tough.

The same jet came back a few days later only minutes before we left the town, maybe he came back to say bye the same way he came to say hi when we first got there! This time the strike was far closer and actually scared the shit out of some of us for a change. We were outside in the street next to the new bakery that we built in the town, which is close to the front (the city is surrounded on two sides, one by a major base, the other by a series of fortified checkpoints) when the Sukhoi circled over us, I could not even see it since it was so high and a little boy, no older than 6 kindly pointed it out to me since he was an expert by now. The jet circled us, then flew over then made another circle and started diving for us, Abu Abdo ran across the road, which offered no more protection than where we already were, and I just stood there and did nothing, it's not that I was frozen scared or stupidly brave, it's just what everyone else was doing, there was basically nothing we could do. You can't outrun a jet, and being inside any building offered no shelter either as it would just fall on us. As the jet came closer a guy I know who is in the FSA named Amir started hopelessly firing at the jet with his ancient anti-aircraft gun mounted on a truck. Mind you, this jet must travel at maybe 700 or 1000kmh, so there is no or very little chance he'd hit it. Then the jet released it's rocket, was a surreal site to see the rocket being released it since all of this is happening in only a few seconds, luckily for us, the rocket went over us and the first thing we heard was the jet over our heads, so close it made the ground shake, then the second thing we heard was the loudest sound I ever heard in my life, one that makes your ears ring for a while afterwards, it was the rocket hitting, thankfully, an empty building a few blocks away.

Mahrouz's younger brother, who just got out from doing 11months in Sadnaya prison in Damascus (because he helped Abu Mahrouz fake some ID papers so he could defect from the army) laughed right after the strike and said to me, "since you heard, it means you're alright!"

To give you an idea of how "normal" this is to people. The airstrikes. About 2 min before the jet struck, a guy from the bakery asks me if I want tea, I say no since I don't eat/drink sugar and in many places in Syria, they boil the tea with the sugar instead of adding it later to individual cups. I denied this guy's offer for tea for a few days, so he says that he's going to make me a pot with no sugar. So sure enough, about 3 min or so after the airstrike, he comes back with the pot of tea and begins to pour for everyone, and then, one by one, outrage hits! The guys, a mix of bakery employees, Mahrouz's family and FSA soldiers are pissed off. Amir, the AA gun operator, takes one sip and is so mad, he puts the cup on the ground and walks away back to his truck (which the gun is stuck to). Amir also mentions to us that he "almost" hit the jet, but that his gun jammed, which is what all AA-gunners say :-) One guy almost dry-heaves and the rest are genuinely pissed that there is no sugar in the tea. The guy that made the tea is getting shit from everyone, he then accuses me of not wanting sugar and then everyone starts berating me for my no-sugar drinking tea habit. I start laughing and then shouted out "Are you guys really more pissed at no sugar in your tea than the Sukhoi jet that just almost killed us!" and they all laugh and say yes. They are used to airstrikes and shelling and death and misery. They are not used to sugarless tea.

A few more minutes after the airstrike, the school (there are still two state-operated schools running in the town) is immediately convened for the day, so children are pouring out into the street. They do this since the school entrance was hit twice by jets in the past and they don't want the risk of all the kids in the school when Assad finally hits it. We then hear the jet again and since there are so many kids in the street, people get serious and start screaming for people to stop gathering since most times, the jet strikes twice. Lucky for everyone, in this town at least, the jet heads off to another close by town and bombs it. Just a side-note on the schools. In many towns that even have schools left (most are bombed by Assad or teachers/students fled) the state is still paying teachers. I asked a friend how it was that the state was paying teachers in the and other liberated towns and that he was fighting Assad at the same time and he said "We are not against the state, we are agains the regime. The state is ours, for the people."

Unfortunately, a day after I leave a helicopter comes to the town and dumps a barrel of TNT onto a building. I'm speaking literally. As simple as that. A helicopter sits over the town and then soldiers in it light a fuse to a crude old barrel stuffed with TNT and it falls onto the town. These barrels can flatten about 2-3 buildings at a time, military geeks (like Brown Moses) have said they have never seen such a tactic used before the Syrian Revolution started. The barrel only kills a small boy and his mother, was miraculous that it did not kill more people. Then again, the town that used to have 150,000 people before the revolution has only about 20,000 or 30,000 now. If there is one thing Syrians hate more than anything, even more than sarin gas, it's these barrels. You watch the helicopter hover overhead. It's so high, AA guns can't reach it (but they still shoot since if they don't locals berate the FSA for 'not doing anything' Amir is always frustrated with this since each AA bullet costs $15). Then you see a small barrel lobbed out the back and it takes about 20 seconds or even more to fall. During this time, people try to run, but since it's so high up, your perception is fooled. You don't know if its falling above you, or 1000m away. You don't know whether to run forward, backward or to the side. You need to guess. If you live in a building, it's not enough time to get downstairs and out, but it's more than enough to hear every screaming "barrrrmeeeeeel!" (barrel) and realize that you will not make it. This is why this specific weapon of Assad is the most hated. The wait before death is the dreaded part. The instant death is one that everyone I know wishes for.

In Mahrouz's town the shelling is also pretty much constant. It just goes on all day and all night. It's the background theme to the town. Some fall far, some near. There is no real target other than the town itself. One day while drinking tea (again) at a friends house, about 20 of us, a shell fell right outside the house, I flinched (more like ducked) and realized that not a single person in the room did. No one even stopped sipping their tea. They did not miss a beat. No one said "oh that was a close one" or "wow, that was loud". It's as if that specific strike never happened. No one asked who was outside or if anyone was hit. It was just normal. And here I am writing an entire paragraph on this single shell while I would bet all the money in the world, not a single person in that room would remember it, maybe just what we ate that day there!

Point of all the writing above is that I can write an essay on an airstrike and a shell strike while the fact of the matter is that both happen every single day, without lull, across much of Syria. It's not a "big" story to news orgs that a barrel was dropped and killed a mother and her son. I mean just yesterday 44 people (all civilians too) in Aleppo were killed when Assad's jets hit three areas, one an open street market. Not a single mention anywhere, although I think I saw it as a blurb on some 'what happened in Syria today' article.

I ran into a guy that was possibly the only foreign reporter in (northern) Syria today. We were in Reyhanli at the time. He works for the [...] Post but was not reporting from them since he told me that all major news organizations have an agreed moratorium/black-out on reporting about and from Northern Syria. This was to discourage their own reporters and freelancers from going into Syria since the wave of kidnappings that got worse in the last few months. This reporter, who I won't name, was having none of that. He said that now more than ever people needed to know what was happening in Syria since Assad essentially had free reign to do as he liked. I thanked him for his courage. He is right in his assessment. The fact that no 'white man' would be there to witness (aka verify) Assad's atrocities or that anything happened ... just plain old Syrian Arabs, whom I suppose don't count as real humans offering real testimonies would mean that nothing would be reported. In the last 3 weeks the reporter had already been to Syria 4 times.

I met another reporter in Reyhanli who came to the prosthetic limbs center, he was from the [...] Times in the UK. He came with an aid org that co-sponsors the center with us. He said his editor forbade him from going into Syria but that he was going to go anyways until the last minute with his hosts in Turkey cancelled and decided not to take him in. Now here is why so many reporters get kidnapped. I repeat this to everyone I know who wants to go to Syria. This reporter was going to go in with a girl who's about 24 and two guys about the same age along with a driver. This is a BAD idea. They had no plans to be escorted by the FSA or any other armed opposition group. Thus, if they rolled up to any random checkpoint, unarmed, loaded with camera equipment and cash, they are easy prey and would be, at best, robbed and worst kidnapped/killed. I think you'd find that most foreign kidnap victims in Syria fit the above scenario, no protection and naive beyond belief. One reporter who was kidnapped months back then escaped wrote in the NYT that he was taken when he decided to take a cab back to Turkey from Aleppo by

HIMSELF! Are you kidding me! Would you take a cab in Mexico by yourself? Or Brazil? Or Pakistan? No.

Anyways, due to the above and the fact that Al Qaida is not making it any better, Assad has had free reign in the press and is winning the media war hands down. Remember when I told you that all he had to do was implant a shadow of a doubt into peoples heads? That's how easy it is for him to negate the fact that he dropped a barrel of TNT on a family ... "would I realllllly do that? c'mon! no one would do that!". So not only does he have that, but he has a de facto monopoly on reporting ... again.

Another of the major changes since I last went in July, one that takes a disproportionate size in the Western media relative to their size, is that Al Qaida (as represented by the Islamic State of Iraq and Syria aka ISIS) is in many more places than when I last came. Last time I went a group called 'Jabhat Al Nusra' aka JAN (The Victory Front) were the 'scary ones' on the side of the opposition, this has changed dramatically since JAN split and spawned ISIS. The fighters of ISIS are almost all foreign and are what you would call the most 'hard-core' extremists. JAN is almost all Syrian and are much more respected and not feared by Syrians. Why is ISIS feared? It's because they have chosen to "rule" many of the towns and villages that the FSA has liberated. And by "rule" I mean it in the same horrible way Assad ruled. It's to the point that many, almost all, people I met and know think that ISIS is a tool of the Assad regime. Same brutal tactics, different clothing.

We stopped at many ISIS checkpoints while driving around. Almost all those that man the checkpoints are foreigners. Many are just kids no older than 15 or 16, black scarfs around their head to hide their identities. They do this because they know what they are doing is wrong, and to instill fear in people. One very frustrating or should I say offensive thing ISIS does is deny entry or even kidnap Syrians for any reason they see fit. I wanted to go to Aleppo, I was told that I could not pass since I did not have my Syrian ID on me. My

Syrian passport that I had would not do. The fact that my family is from Aleppo would not do. Now how about that? Some Tunisian guy in Syria denies me entry to my city????! Syrians are fed up with them (ISIS). They don't like them and they can't tolerate them anymore. When ISIS first came, they fought and they repaired water and electricity stations, gave out bread for free, gave out cash and wiped out many fake-revolutionary groups that robbed people. However, in hind-sight this was a charade in order to take power. Can you blame Syrians for letting them in the first place as no one came to help us? Now the FSA cannot take them on since its impossible to fight Assad in front and ISIS in the back. It seems that after Assad gassed Syrians with sarin, his standing improved remarkably in the international community and Al Qaida celebrated the "no-strike" by Obama just as much as Assad did.

I could give you a summary of all the other stuff I saw. I could go on about all the injured. The poor. The crippled. The diseased. The miserable. I could talk about the stories Mahrouz's younger brother told me about his 11 months in Assad's prison hell. I could tell you about who died and who survived since my last trip. I could tell you how there is no real international aid effort anywhere. I could go on about how the FSA is being forcibly marginalized and helplessly watching Al Qaida occupy and oppress our liberated towns. But I've already said these stories too many times to too many people and decided it won't make any difference to say them again.

When Mahrouz's younger brother started talking to me about his torture and the ungodly things that they did to him in prison, I felt ashamed. Not for the fact that he went through it and I did not, but for the fact that I did not really want to listen because I was not bothered to. I've heard so many similar accounts from so many people that we are desensitized. It's normal to have had electric cables placed in your mouth and genitalia. It's normal to have been starved to 1/2 your original body weight. It's normal to have shared a 3x3m room with 120 people for almost a year. It's normal to watch cellmates chosen at random to be executed. Assad desensitized us. He stole our emotions from us. A guy told me how after his brother was killed in Homs and they buried him, that 3 days later he broke down crying. Not because his brother was dead (his father and another brother were killed some weeks earlier) but because he realized he did not cry at all and it scared him.

I don't have a vision of what a solution would look like in the future. I feel like vomiting whenever someone says "What about the Geneva talks?". They might as well be conducted on Mars between a Canadian and a Japanese. It means nothing to anyone Syria. To think Assad will negotiate his own departure is ludicrous. To think Syrians will sit down at a table with their would-be executioner is offensive. I don't know what Syria will look like in a year or in 10 years. I don't know what would be the best for the most people. All of these are things I thought I once knew, but now I do not.

What I do know is that the fighters battling against Assad will do so until the last bullet. There is no 'going back' for them. Not now, not ever. For civilians, most just want an income. They want the pride of working again to earn their living instead of begging and not even coming close to making ends meet. In the cities that Assad still occupies, residents pay local FSA brigades to not attack Assad's forces in the town. At least this is the case in Hama, where a good friend of mine who I meet on my trips to Syria lives (he lives in the suburbs). They (the citys residents) have been given two choices by Assad. Either live under his oppression or to face the same fate as Homs or Aleppo, razed to the ground or even face the fate of Raqqa, to be ruled by Al Qaida. When faced with the choice to live or die, most will choose life even though it's not much of a life.

I have no doubt in my mind, not a single one, that Assad and his regime will fall one day. When, I do not know. But they will fall. The areas Assad has lost will never submit to him again. Even if they are re-occupied, they will never submit. What I also now realize is that even when Assad is gone, he succeeded in his 'Assad or we burn the country' motto often repeated by his supporters (it rhymes in Arabic). Assad has opened the flood gates to tens upon tens of thousands of mercenaries and ultra-sectarian militias to come fight for him. This cannot be easily reversed. You can call me biased, but I only report what I see on the ground and hear from my friends and family, for all the fuss over Al Qaida in Syria, and don't misunderstand me, they are brutal and horrible and are hurting us, they are few and far between, far far fewer than Assad's own foreign extremists. It's just that the media finds a 'better' story or to be more accurate, a much more lazy 'easy' story to report on Al Qaida. I mean, you'd think that Syria is all Al Qaida if you watch the news today. I'd say maybe less than 10,000, and that's being generous.

So with all this gloom we still carry on doing what we do. We opened a bakery on my last trip, delivered 3 ambulances and marked a spot to dig a new water well. I'm working on getting a 3D printer for the prosthetic limb center to print cheap "robohands". I'm also trying to find charities in the US to help me build solar 'micro-grids' to get power back to people since diesel is expensive. We are also working on larger projects to filter water and build many more water wells. We also have a lot of medical equipment coming in December that will be distributed to about 12 hospitals in Northern Syria. I'm also moving more towards development projects rather than pure aid-handouts. As I said, people want to work, and since the Syrian expat community only operates small aid orgs like ours, we cannot afford to hand out food to millions, we need the UN, which is non-existant in Northern Syria. We just need to keep on doing what we do. To show our family and friends in Syria we will never give up on them and to show Assad that after each bomb he drops, we will come back to rebuild again and again and again.

--A.F.

P.S. I forgot to mention to you that the guy wearing the pink sorority pledge shirt in Atmeh (FSA that protects the camp) that we met died a few weeks back. I forgot to mention it to you earlier since when someone told me (while I was in Syria) I forgot about it until now for some reason. I don't even remember his name, I guess that's how sad it's become (ie, how frequent people die). I also did not ask how he died. They simply said "Yeah, that guy was martyred" when I asked about him. "Martyred" in Syria means he died at the hands of Assad forces. Don't mean to bum you out about it, and you should not be since this is what is now normal in Syria. Instead of being sad now we usually say "hamdullah" when someone dies. It means "Thank God".

Final Dispatch
~ Sent December 28th, 2013

At the end of summer 2012, after weeks spent in Bolivia shadowing doctors distributing bio-sand filters to indigenous families up and down the Rio Beni, I decided to take the bus to Peru for my last few days in South America. The bus was delayed several hours because the Peruvian teachers went on strike and, apparently, had put boulders in Peru's major roads. This proved an effective way to get attention through forcing gridlock, and we arrived in Cuzco at 2am instead of 4pm. I piled in a cab with three nineteen-year-olds, one cheerful Irish girl and a lovely couple from London. The couple hadn't made reservations anywhere. The Irish girl had made one at a place called the Wild Rover, and I had made one at a slightly less youth-oriented establishment in the old town, where the night attendant had fallen so soundly asleep that multiple calls with the cabbie's phone and rings of the bell weren't enough to rouse him.

So, all four of us went to the Wild Rover, a hostel whose wifi password was "party2012", if that gives you any idea. The Wild Rover boasted four beds left in a twelve-bed room. Absolutely no one was in the other eight beds. They were downstairs, at 80s night.

The young man from the couple, both of whom came from Indian immigrant families in London, padded by in his boxers, his skinny feet barely making noise as he opened the bathroom door.

He shut it again.

"Um," he said.

We looked up.

"I can't go in there," he said, eyes wide. "One of you has to—it's just—go look."

He looked perplexedly at me, and I realized that at twenty-eight I was *old* to him.

So I braved the bathroom door.

There sat a girl on the toilet, pants around her ankles, fast asleep, drooling on her knees. Her hair was still in a sideways ponytail and the purple glitter on her eyelids was smeared on her knees, mixing with the drool.

And that's when it hit me: I was indeed older. I was not the girl passed out in the bathroom! I may have been that girl's rough equivalent in my early twenties, but I was the one helping her up now (with the help of the Irish girl) as she groaned at us please to just leave her there. I remembered how terrible the spins are when you've had so much that you pass out before you meant to. We pulled her pants up and left her standing because she was not about to take a step. She gripped the sink as we closed the door. The four of us brushed our teeth with water from our water bottles, splashing it on our faces. As I put my old-lady earplugs in, I saw the British boy creep into his girlfriend's bunk, where they proceeded to sleep like kittens, in a familiar knot.

I often recalled that night over the following summer, when I stayed in the same hostel in Istanbul, in Taksim, each time I came through before heading out to the Syrian border or to Nairobi. The only person who was more of a fixture than I was was a drop-dead gorgeous twenty-year-old boy with olive skin and dark eyes, plus a wicked grin. Like a Middle Eastern Antonio Banderas. His name was Nicolas. My first night in the hostel, a group trouped out the door as I returned from a water bottle buying mission and invited me along to go hear live music. Nicolas was among them, and his English was good enough for him to make jokes in.

Taksim even on a regular evening is bustling, and the summer of 2013 was an eventful one there. Gezi park had just been saved, and the protesters were gone. Back in late June, the only evidence of the violent protests were the yellow tape still bordered Gezi park and the police wearing reflective yellow vests who gathered in a tent nearby. Our group included possibly one of the most ebullient people I've ever met, an American-raised guy from Texas who was born to Turkish parents, and the Turkish girl whose company he was keeping after meeting her out a few nights before. There was also a foxy girl from Iran with tons of black eyeliner, a mop of burgandy hair, and tiny jean shorts who worked at the hostel in what seemed an exceedingly casual arrangement—as I came and went over the course of the summer, she would have quit the hostel, but still be staying there, then come to work again to afford a room at a nearby apartment, then returned to Iran, then come again—and a tiny American girl who was about to start a full ride to study art at Kalamazoo and who escorted me one warm afternoon to buy cigarette rolling materials at a kiosk in one of the cobbled streets. I would prove so bad at rolling them that I effectively quit smoking cigarettes, aside from those Nicolas and company would give me.

Nicolas loved the ebullient American guy, and vice versa. As we waited for beers and the Turkish liquor called Raki that turns a cloudy light blue with ice, they did this hilarious—and, according to them, traditional--dance where they appeared to pass an invisible ball back and forth by jutting a chin or an elbow out to each other in time with the music. As we headed back to the hostel, where breakfast wasn't even served until 10am and the cobbled street below never slept, Nicolas grinned at the American guy, who had hoisted his giggling girl-friend over his shoulder. "You know it's going to be great time, when you go out with him, because of his attitude," Nicolas said to me. "If you decide it's going to be great, it will. He decides it will be a good time."

Nicolas had, I believe, one of the single rooms way up on the fourth floor of the narrow Mystic Hostel. In late July, on the fourth of my five stints in Istanbul, the Iranian girl was smoking cigarettes by the front window of the lobby, where people would gather in the evenings to throw one back before hitting the streets. More protests had elapsed while I was gone. While I had already felt the sunscreen-type-burn in my eyes that denoted clashes nearby while walking around Taksim, soon I would finally be on the main drag, Istiklal, for actual shots fired by the police at young people with kerchiefs over their mouths.

"There's been more tear gas, right?" I asked the Iranian girl.

She nodded, exhaling smoke. "I could see them, running right under this window," she said, "and some of them couldn't see where they were going. We had to put the window cover up because it was hurting our eyes even in here."

She looked even more gorgeous, if that was possible, and when Nicolas came downstairs, I saw his shock of dark curls was slicked back. I'd come and gone so many times that I knew this was a noticeable change in his appearance. The lobby filled, and I realized why both Nicolas and the Iranian girl were dressing up: they were dressing up for each other. That night during a live performance I asked her whether there was perhaps a romance going on and she shrugged impishly. There were a lot of us that night, dancing on the fourth floor balcony of a building, and Nicolas nuzzled both the Iranian girl and yet another American girl they both seemed very friendly with.

Nicolas was, like every human his age with a smartphone, constantly on Facebook. I talked to him on it recently for this work, because Nicolas was the only thing that made sense, given his indefinite amount of time living in a hostel in Istanbul with not too much to do and no agenda full of palaces to see, the only thing it made sense for him to be, with no plans to trek to the coast and no family around: he was a Syrian refugee. He used Facebook to communicate with his friends back home in Damascus.

He was one of the two million people who had managed to make it out. He was lucky enough to have the means to stay in a hostel and not on the street, lucky enough to have escaped Damascus, where his family lived: triply lucky, in fact, because his family is Christian. That family was, for the most part, in Germany, where his sister had been living for years. Nicolas was killing time, waiting for the German embassy to let him travel there and see his mother and father and sister again. He told me his peers were still going to university, and that people had decided to live even if bombs were dropping nearby. I wondered how Nicolas would remember this epoch in his life. Was time standing still for him? Did his "lost weekend" at this hostel in Istanbul, during a summer of clashes and romance with a red-haired girl, take on its own life, and stop feeling only like a transition? Someday, perhaps, I will ask him.

Part of the reason it has been hard for me to sit down and write this piece is that Nicolas is one of two million people who have the right to tell us directly what this living hell, the one that the international community hasn't stopped, was, is, and will be like. We will be paying for this for the rest of my lifetime; like Gitmo, it's one of the first nails in my coffin of responsibility vis a vis the body politic. I'm officially older than my hostel-mates, older than half world's population, at the ripe age of twenty-nine. My generation will deal with our inaction, the turning of the world's back to this, for the rest of our lives. One million children, some with shrapnel in their stomachs, some legless, orphaned, destitute, begging in the streets in Lebanon and Jordan: we will hear their stories, steadily, over the next half-century, and I am dreadfully certain that we will see, in the actions of one million children grown into adults who remember how no one helped them, the violence and utter misery that is the legacy of severe trauma gone unchecked, unabated, and unaddressed.

This may be the first time, because the entire international community could view the videos coming out of Syria and because the United Nations existed, that ignored children in Congo and Syria will be literally correct in the emotional "hyperbole" that *no one in the world* cares about them. We will hear from them, hopefully in books not that I write but that *they* write, and movies and lectures and panels they make and speak in. But we will hear from them whether we like the way they express themselves or not. One million abandoned children, with no help out of hell, are one million people with good reason to turn to fundamentalism and violence. And the violence already suffered has broken the hearts of all Syrians who once lived in Syria and who can't anymore. "The last three years was like hell to every Syrian in the world," Nicolas typed to me in a Facebook chat in October:

"The ugly ways of killing from both sides the fact that your life will be like hell when you lose safe in your country ..walking in the street and looking at cars and expecting any one of them to explode any time
The falling bombs and snipers
You know you could die any second bit your worst nightmares when car explode and you read the death list just this one second of hoping not to read a family member name...I left Damascus cuz its too dangerous and simply o don't want to die I am not ready yet and had enough blood
But the terrible thing is when you discover that you are just politics for the big countrys and no body care about you and the worst of that Iam less human than there people
I spent two years of my life not asking much just to get a visa to be safe and see my family over there"

His words rang heavy bells: it's what my Jewish grandmother went through after fleeing to America in World War Two, reading the lists of the dead out of the camps in Poland, where her (German) family had been sent. Only one sister made it out, unable to bear children. No one knows exactly how it felt to be my grandmother, reading that one name on the list, meeting my great-aunt at the dock, but Syrians might have the best idea.

The other bell was that Nicolas echoed every single other young Syrian I heard from, of any religion: that the message was that they are less than human, that they are not human in the eyes of the world. I remember learning the word "dehumanization": I learned it in high school, when we studied the Holocaust and World War Two. Dehumanized people commit inhuman acts. Sometimes the abuse comes from a parent in childhood. Sometimes it comes from the world at large. But it is abuse, this blood on our hands, and blood will be paid for it as the years unfold. World War Three has happened – to Syrians.

Nicolas wrote further:

"Like one year ago I went to malizia to apply to avisa to see to see my sister there but I got rejected and I appealed and got rejected also
I had to stay two months over there
Then I came back to Syria and it was spook dangerous thing was hard over there a bomb landed 50 m away from my house
Then I went to Istanbul with my father and grand father to apply to visa to attend my sis wedding and also got rejected me and my grand father but my father got the visa
…I came back to Syria for a week and then came back to Istanbul and I said I will try to get visa for the last time and also got rejected but I was trying to find some one to smuggle me to germany
To go illegally
But it didn't work out it was so expensive and risky
I believe no human should be illegal"

Nicolas was initially for the opposition, and wanted Assad out, but by summer 2013, the skies had already turned dark for the Christian Syrian minority: Jihadists, the ISIS, Al-Quaeda and Hezbollah affiliates, from Kuwait, from Iran, from Saudi Arabia, had descended upon Syria, its war, and its civilians, "liberating" towns from Assad only to enforce their own extremist, oppressive forms of Islamic law. Nicolas and the initial victims of Assad's atrocities in the face of peaceful protest wanted *democracy*. The guys who had assumed the mantle of "opposition" were the opposite of that: they wanted Assad out, too, but they essentially wanted him out because they thought he was too *liberal*. It's not unlike people wanting to oust Hitler for being too tolerant. *Those* are the guys mostly running Syria's "liberated" areas now, because those are the guys getting enough money from largely private donors in the gulf countries for food and effective weapons. The original opposition—the ones who wanted democracy—are fighting both Assad and the Jihadists, and basically no one's helping them. Their numbers dwindle daily. Just now, over Christmas, as Assad's forces pretty much carpet-bombed part of Aleppo with, literally, *barrels* of explosives, their numbers dwindled even faster than usual. As Abu Faisal has articulated, the tiny, ad hoc, risky business of aid within Syria's orders, of attempting to clothe freezing Syrians and provide infant formula, is arguably for naught when the people wearing those clothes die the next day from barrel bombs.

"So that's when I discovered the the human rights is a lie
And no body caer if you are with your family or not
And now Iam in Lebanon and my family got me some thing
like family reunion so I will get my visa in 1 November

I spent over 20 thousand dollars just going to malizia istanbul
from embassy to embassy
And get rejected
My father selled the house the care and a lot of things to keep
me safe
And basically we don't have any thing left there

Just our emotions and memories"

"I wanted Assad out, but now, I want the government much more than the rebels at any checkpoint," Nicolas told me once, after a night out as we sat on the sofa in the hostel lobby. "I think when I get to Germany I need to see a person for therapy, because the videos of beheading Christians make me so scared."

He produced his phone for his pocket to show me a video, but it wasn't a clip of jihadists beheading priests. He wanted to show me "the most brave person": the commander who came to talk to the opposing army, who put down his gun, said something along the lines of, "I'm Syrian and you're Syrian, we all love Syria, we shouldn't be fighting."

"That has to be the most courage, in that video, that man doing that," Nicolas said emphatically. "They could have killed him."

Like the skinny young man roughly Nicolas's age in a hand-me-down pink california sorority t shirt whom I met in in Syria's Atmeh refugee camp, who sat with us and made sure nothing happened to us as we waited for the car that would bring us back from the border to Reyhanli, that courageous commander is now dead.

I was just in the Santa Barbara mountains, close to the ranch where I grew up, for Winter Solstice. My first quarter in a PhD program was like a vortex of stress about texts and papers that didn't ultimately matter, a vortex characterized by that peculiar province of academics in the humanities: egos that grow mightier the fewer people know or care about your theories. I was admonished for "crossing a line" when I ventured the suggestion that my professor could choose another tactic than making students cry repeatedly during seminar break in front of their peers. "You can't tell them how to do their job," my department head told me. "He can tell you how to be, because he's your professor and that's what professors do."

It's rare for me to be speechless, but I was. I seem unable to swallow the "this is how you play the game" tradition of pandering to authority that isn't handled well when the stakes are so low and the people involved have cars, roofs, and dentists. After receiving those pearls of wisdom from my department head, I drove my dented van to a compound off the grid in the Los Padres Mountain range where my Chumash surrogate dad lives with his family in houses they built. This man, T, was also my Aikido instructor, and he's known me over half my life, since before I ever left America, since before I ever had sex or participated in a protest. I bring T carved owls from each country I work in. They live in nooks in his earthen house. I am technically agnostic, but I do believe that

I've survived my sometimes-dicey experiences abroad because T sends a pack of guardian angels to watch over me, bouncer angels with the brawn of Mr. Clean. We call T's home "the mountain", and I go to the mountain regularly. I brought my grandmother's ashes there, driving them down from Lummi Island, WA, before leaving for the summer on the trip that included a tour of the refugee camp in Syria. I left her on the hill good for watching sunsets, and imagine her there, faint against the sky as a photo slide in a daylit room. On December 21st, T led the Winter Solstice ceremony, informing those twelve of us gathered there that his work was difficult, but that he was the only one around who knew how to do it: how to open the West Gate to the valley of the shadow, where the spirits of the dead live. He warned us that the spirits of the dead would heed our prayers but especially because we were speaking in English we needed to be very specific. "Don't just ask for every person on earth to have water," he told us, "because you might end up with a monsoon. And sometimes the spirits can be frightening when they visit, so be prepared for that." The next morning in the blue of dawn I awakened and walked to the cook shack, where T sat with some coffee. He had charcoal smeared on his face, and explained to me: "At first light, just now, I performed the ceremony that closes the gate once again, the one to the west, and I had to disguise myself, so I'm not taken."

Over the course of the first five hours of the circle (which were all I stayed awake for), after we all stood and threw tobacco into the flames, the fire burned and people drummed and we could come and go from the circle at will. Inside the cook shack, we feasted. I had attempted apple pie from scratch and was delighted when T's stepdaughter, a chef – who happens also to be the first (and not the last, though I didn't mention my bisexuality to my Atmeh companions) girl I ever had sex with – after she convinced me to join her boyfriend and her one night in her earthen house about two hundred feet away), was shocked that I had made the crust myself. I'm an over-sensitive, clumsy, anxious, confused bimbo a lot of the time in America, and few of my close friends here can reconcile how I survive my stints working in far-flung places after watching me try to do laundry, keep track of my wallet, or cut garlic correctly. None of the people in the far-flung places know much of my sexually and politically liberal upbringing or the zebra ranch I grew up on, either. I bring my own history to bear in this narrative not for shock value, but because it is significant that my "bedfellows" in the trip to Syria were of a culture and religion that would condemn a great many of my personal choices and beliefs—that among the Syrian men who escorted me to the camp, the brain underneath the green pashmina I used as a headscarf harbored memories of sex, drugs, and protests that went without context in a place like Atmeh and that rendered me a habitual violator of the customs held dear by my hosts themselves. The opposite was also true, in a way, and the resultant amoeba-ness possibly what writing serves, among other things, to provide an outlet or tenuous resolution for. So, I asked T whether I could bring my journal by the fire and write what I had to say to the spirits. I was thinking of what I wished for the children at Atmeh, specifically, the girl with the dark eyes whose picture I had decided not to take. I didn't want to get it wrong.

In response, T held up a mason jar and looked at me through it, so he blurred.

"That would be like this," he said. "Why make it harder for the spirits to hear you?"

I nodded, and didn't ask why we needed to be so specific with our words if words were an obstacle.

No spirits visited me in any frightening way for the first few hours, and I thought perhaps simply they wouldn't. Then that night, my phone downloaded a message from Abu Faisal: Mahrouz, the larger-than-life cardiologist who was always absconding with vegetables for us to eat during our days in Reyhanli, whose booming voice made lewd jokes and who, along with his brothers, was the de facto leader of the village of Maaret al Nouman, had been kidnapped by the ISIS eight days prior. He had not wanted to give in to them because if he did, the civilians of Maaret would be subject to the law of the ISIS, one of the Al-Quaeda affiliate "rebel" groups. I had no context for what might be happening to Mahrouz at that moment—were they torturing him? Was he cold? Did he have shelter? – and thought mainly of his fifteen-year-old daughter, one of his three girls, who was so recognizably teenage in her beauty and awkwardness, who had come with us into Atmeh, and who probably was much less young after this week. He was meeting with ISIS to suss out some conflicts between them and the civilians of Maaret, and when things got heated, the ISIS bodyguards took him. Dr. Mahrouz is stubborn, with expansive hospitality and expansive humor and a belly laugh, and he chose not to give in to the "rebels" whom the media knows as the now de facto face of the opposition. I crept to T's stepdaughter's house, and slept in one of the little nooks in the corner, somehow unable to bring these ghosts to the fire. Dr. Mahrouz's booming voice. The warm sun shining through the leaves of vegetables in his hands. His jokes about Angelina Jolie.

I slept until the blue of dawn, falling to sleep in a jumble of images of the doctor and the night before Solstice, when one young man, another "child" of T's who lives on the mountain with his wife and two sons, made a fire as part of his monthly fasting ritual on the patio. A few of us joined him, warming our hands and feet as the stars appeared beyond the oak branches. The ranches around where I grew up have the most stars in their skies out of anywhere, anywhere in the world I've ever seen, even the skies above the Mongolian tundra in winter. The young father's younger son, who is two, clambered onto his dad's lap as we talked and Bamboo, the kitty with a dog's personality, puddled into purrs in the boy's lap, so they were a father-son-kitty pile melting together by the fire. I looked at the clear night sky, and at the boy sandwiched between a purring cat and his father bending over him, and I thought this is what every child deserves and so few of them get. And so I was already thinking of them, of the children who followed us around in the dry heat at Atmeh, with dirty skin and fathomless eyes, with candy bars to sell us or empty bottles to jump on and frighten us with the gunshot noise that only we weren't used to, when the young father asked: what's the most intense experience you've ever had?

If it's not my suffering, but merely witnessing the suffering of others, how intense is it? What is intensity in human life, and how is it measured? But those weren't the questions I was asking. I thought about "experience". I wondered when an experience begins and ends. I could say, the day I went in for an IUD insertion and they couldn't put it in because I was twelve days pregnant, the feeling I had then, or the poem I wrote to the unborn child I wasn't ready for, whose mother wouldn't have a house, a viable income, or a spouse. Or how that poem was plagiarized by the would-be father, lines from it sent off as part of his poem that he was trying to have published without my knowledge. But where does that experience begin and end? Sex is an intense thing, and it's what made the fertilization, so would that experience begin there, and end with the writhing on a gurney and a mound of blood in a dixie cup? Or would it end with the work I ended up beginning in 2011 with refugee women from Congo in Nairobi, and how I believe the spirit of the person I asked to wait and come back again when I was ready to bear children is what guided me and made me able to do that work, work with girls who don't have mothers of their own anymore and whom I wouldn't have traveled to Africa to meet if I'd had a ten-month-old child? Where does the most intense experience of my life begin and end? I went to Atmeh camp just inside Syria on the three-year anniversary of my due date. I went into Atmeh and looked into the eyes of these children, some of whom may now be dead of explosives or hunger or cold, on the due date of the baby I didn't bear. Does the experience end there? Does it end in the marble-dark eyes of the most beautiful girl I have ever seen, the one I wrote to you about before, who reminded me of Sharbat (the famous face described by Mindy Kaling as "the National Geographic girl with the intense eyes")?

At the fire I didn't speak of my own child. I spoke of the ones who already came into the world, and who might already be dead. I said that the knowledge that I would leave and continue living a comfortable, rewarding life and that these children could not leave that place among the olive trees engendered a feeling I don't think there are words for.

It's not my suffering, and I've said more than my piece. Now I believe it is time for me to listen.

Ming

NOTE: Yesterday Mahrouz was released – and I misunderstood Abu Faisal's email: it was the other Mahrouz, his brother who was taken, the one who heads the local army, and whose children are even younger than the Doctor Mahrouz's.
   Nicolas is in Germany with his family.

44166532R00064

Made in the USA
Charleston, SC
20 July 2015